When
Smart Kids
Underachieve
in School

T0386574

When Smart Kids Underachieve in School

Practical Solutions for Teachers

Todd Stanley

Routledge
Taylor & Francis Group

NEW YORK AND LONDON

Library of Congress Cataloging-in-Publication Data

Names: Stanley, Todd, author.
Title: When smart kids underachieve in school : practical solutions for
  teachers / by Todd Stanley.
Description: Waco, Texas : Prufrock Press Inc., [2018] | Includes
  bibliographical references.
Identifiers: LCCN 2017031920|
 Subjects: LCSH: Academic achievement--Psychological aspects. | Motivation in
  education. | Teacher-student relationships.
Classification: LCC LB1062.6 .S77 2018 | DDC 371.2/85--dc23
LC record available at https://lccn.loc.gov/2017031920

First published in 2018 by Prufrock Press Inc.

Published in 2021 by Routledge
605 Third Avenue, New York, NY 10017
2 Park Square, Milton Park, Abingdon, Oxon OX14 4RN

Routledge is an imprint of the Taylor & Francis Group, an informa business.

Cover design by Raquel Trevino and layout design by Allegra Denbo

ISBN: 9781032143569 (hbk)
ISBN: 9781618217035 (pbk)

DOI: 10.4324/9781003239567

Table of Contents

Part I

INTRODUCTION

The Story of Mike

I was working with a group of fourth-grade students when I felt a vibration in my pocket. At lunch when I checked my phone, I found the following text message:

Just wanted to let you know I am joining the army.

It was from a number I did not recognize, so I texted back congratulating the person but also asking to identify him- or herself. The message came back:

This is Mike.

Mike? My Mike? Why would he be joining the army, and at age 28?

Mike and I go way back—he was a seventh grader when I was a teacher just 3 years into my career. I remember Mike coming into my class with a knit cap on that proudly displayed KISS across its brow. If it were the 1970s, this would have been appropriate, because KISS was huge then. This, however, was the 1990s—not a good sign. He had a little bit of an attitude, was kind of a smart aleck, but was not anything that even a rookie teacher such as myself could not handle. This was not the case for all of his teachers, however. When our team of teachers got together to discuss how the school year was going, one of the veteran teachers complained about Mike.

"He is always questioning my authority," she noted.

"What do you mean 'questioning'?" I asked.

"Whenever I teach a lesson, he always questions me on it. I think he is trying to make me look stupid."

"Sounds to me like he is just curious."

As the year rolled on, I never had any issues with Mike being disrespectful, although he did like to ask questions—sometimes relentlessly—like a machine gun firing. But they were usually an attempt to dig a little deeper and benefitted everyone in the class.

Luckily for me, we looped the students for 2 years, and I had Mike for his eighth-grade year as well. The most rewarding part about having students over multiple years, especially in junior high, is that you get to see them grow up right in front of you. They go from little kids to the young men and women they will grow up to be, both physically and mentally. I grew pleased with how seriously Mike was beginning to take his academics. I saw bright things for his future. During these 2 years, I learned Mike's father had passed away when he was just a young child. As happens to a lot of male teachers who teach younger grades, for many of the students, I was the first male teacher they ever had. Because of this, I had the added privilege of being a male role model for students, especially ones like Mike who did not have one at home. I also discovered that he was gifted across the board, testing gifted in all four subject areas as well as superior cognitive ability, meaning he was highly gifted. His questions were not meant to challenge authority; he was just naturally inquisitive.

By the time he finished his eighth-grade year, Mike had become my favorite student. I know teachers are not supposed to pick favorites, but we do, and Mike and I had a bond that was stronger than just student and teacher. A couple of years later, I was working for a humanities program that recruited juniors and seniors from local high schools to a magnet program. I went to Mike's school, and he was first in line to join. This meant another 2 years with Mike, and by this time he had matured from a KISS-wearing miscreant to a thoughtful young man who wrote poetry and played the guitar. The intelligence he had used to flummox veteran teachers had morphed into a desire to learn at a deeper level and produce amazing work.

Near the beginning of his senior year, Mike asked me to write him a letter of recommendation as he was applying to Harvard University. I was more than happy to do so and gushed about Mike and his wonderful abilities that I had the chance to witness over 4 years time. He was accepted and began attending the Ivy League school the next year.

I felt as though Mike was living up to his potential and was going to set the world on fire with his accomplishments.

It was during that year on Thanksgiving that my phone rang. It was Mike. He was having doubts about being at Harvard and was having trouble finding his place there. I assured him that he was in the right place and that he would be able to accomplish so many great things if he stuck with it. He graduated from Harvard 4 years later.

At this point, Mike and I had become friends. We met for lunch one afternoon, and I asked him what he was doing with himself. He had begun working for a company that refinished basements. I wondered if he was working in the accounting department, designing their website, or even managing projects. Nope, he was just refinishing basements. Now, the world needs people to refinish their basements, but this seemed like something a kid like Mike did while in college, not after he had graduated from one of the most prestigious schools in the nation.

Over the next few years, Mike and I would occasionally get together for lunch, and each time he was still working for the basement company. Then, a couple of years went by until the text about joining the army. Don't get me wrong: Going into the army is a choice that many fine men and women make. But, with his intellectual abilities and skillset, I expected Mike to become the national Poet Laureate, a university professor, or even a high school literature teacher. But alas, we do not get to pick the pathways of our students. We can only try to prepare them for as many of those pathways as possible and hope for the best. The world is full of valedictorians working at gas stations and dropouts who run their own successful businesses.

Would I term Mike an underachiever? He certainly had the potential to be one in junior high. If he had grown too bored, not been challenged, or run into too many teachers who did not allow him to ask so many questions, he might have fallen into that category. Was he an underachiever in his job? That depends on how you look at it—although not many people with advanced abilities or degrees from Harvard work construction unless their name is Will Hunting. Were I Mike's parent, would I want more for him? Certainly. As parents we always want more for our children. The same goes for teachers and their students. Was joining the army underachieving? Again, given Mike's skillset and the life ambitions he had shared with me over the years, it did not seem like a good fit. It seemed more like the act of someone who did not know what to do with his life. As a teacher who worked with him for years, I did not believe it would use his potential to its greatest, which is what we want for every student, not just our favorites.

As teachers, we are challenged on a daily basis to get students to achieve to their fullest potential. This is a daunting task, but it can be even more of a challenge when working with gifted students. By definition, they have the greatest academic potential of all. For example, if a student comes into a sixth-grade mathematics class and is learning at a sixth-grade level, the teacher simply has to prepare him for the seventh grade, the path of most students. If the student comes into a sixth-grade class but can do mathematics on a 10th-grade level, however, the teacher is challenged with getting that student ready for 11th-grade math in order to show a year's growth. Many students underachieve, but because gifted students have so much academic potential, the underachievement can be much greater.

How does a teacher prevent a gifted student from underachieving? Are there signs of underachievement? What about strategies that can be used to combat this scourge of academia? Those are the questions this book will seek to answer. After reading this book, you will have a better understanding of what causes students to underachieve and how to help them to achieve at the level they are capable. This book begins by discussing how many students fall into this category and why this is a serious concern. This is followed by profiles of underachieving gifted students. The subsequent chapters look at the 10 most common causes of underachievement and practical solutions to get students back on track. The book concludes with why it is so important to get gifted students to reach their potential.

Available online is an allegory called "The Unopened Gift" (available at https://myedexpert.com/item/the-unopened-gift-part-1) that provides reasons why students underachieve and what can happen as a result. This can be read to students, parents, and colleagues in order to spark conversation about underachievement.

How Can Someone So Smart Underachieve?

By definition, gifted students are smart. When students are identified gifted by school districts, they have typically performed in the top 5% or higher as compared to all of the other students who took a norm-referenced test. That means they have the potential to be the brightest amongst their peers. Given that they are smart, gifted students always do well in school, which is an environment designed for smart people to thrive, correct? Not so fast on that one. Children identified as gifted do not always make for the best students. There are other factors that play into good grades, such as motivation, effort, interaction, participation, completion of work, being organized, and test-taking and study skills, among others. Just because someone is intelligent does not mean he will apply this to his academics. In fact, he may use his intelligence to avoid schoolwork, getting by on his natural ability, rather than developing the skills needed to be successful in a school setting. This type of student is an underachiever.

Definition of Underachievement

One place to start when defining the term *underachievement* is more clearly defining what it means to be an underachiever. In the current educational environment of data and testing, everything can be evaluated, measured, predicted, and/or disseminated. Yet, determining whether a child is an underachiever is not something you would call a measureable goal. There is not a test that can determine if a student is an underachiever. Instead, it is something that presents itself in spurts and glimpses, and by the time the student is correctly identified as underachieving, it might be too late to get him back on track. Many times, in fact, underachievement is in the eye of the beholder. A student in one class could be perceived as performing well above his peers, and yet in another class, he is considered to be average or even falling behind. What is the true indicator of the achievement of which this student is capable?

Dowdall and Colangelo (1982) described three underlying themes in the definition of gifted underachievement:

1. underachievement as a discrepancy between *potential* achievement and actual achievement,
2. underachievement as a discrepancy between *predicted* achievement and actual achievement, and
3. underachievement as a failure to develop or use potential.

Grades are a typical measure of achievement. If a student receives an A in a class, she is performing at a high level, but if that student is earning a C, she might only be at a basic level. The problem is that grades can be very subjective. This is something that teachers do not like to admit very often, but grading lacks something that every standardized test must have: reliability. This is the ability to perform at a level and achieve a certain score, and then if the student repeats the same performance, he should receive the same score. This is not always the case with grades. The element of bias, whether positive or negative, can factor into grades, or you may have a teacher who places a lot of emphasis on effort and not mastery. If a teacher takes off points because something is turned in late, is that evaluating that student's ability to show what he has learned, or is it more of a reflection of that student's lack of responsibility, not a skill being measured by a standard? Grades do not always reflect a true picture of the achievement of a student.

Another problem is that a student can be getting A's but may not be reaching his full potential. Gifted students can easily become efficient with their effort. School can turn into a game of doing enough to get the desired grade, but not really pushing oneself to the highest levels of one's abilities. Let us be honest: Pushing oneself all of the time can be exhausting. No one wants to make more work for himself than necessary, so if you can figure out a way to get a good grade without having to give it your best, many times this is the route you will take.

As teachers, we get a pretty good sense of what students are capable of. The trick is challenging these students enough so that they are willing to push themselves to the levels where they are stretching their potential.

There are a lot of gray areas that can make the identification of underachievers difficult. For example, a gifted student might exceed expectations in one subject area, but because of a lack of interest or confidence, does not do well in another. Sometimes underachievement can even be related to the teacher rather than the subject. A student might be the best math student in a fourth-grade class, but due to a teacher's style or even a personality conflict, she might struggle in fifth-grade math. Some teachers see gifted students as intimidating or think they are showing signs of disrespect by questioning what goes on in the classroom. Students, however, find it difficult to grow in an environment where they are condemned for stretching their thinking.

Other times the student might have the ability but lacks the confidence, making the issue a social-emotional one. A student might test gifted in math but is told that girls typically do not do well in this subject, and she actually begins to believe it. Or someone who does not like to be criticized is not willing to show his talents as a writer for fear of being told he is no good. It can sometimes turn into a self-fulfilling prophecy, as a gifted student gets a bad grade and then comes to believe that he can do no right. Why bother trying? If students develop this self-concept, it can be very difficult for them to prevent themselves from continuing to spiral downward.

It can also be a challenge to, well, you know, challenge students. As teachers, we walk a fine line between pushing our students to the next level and pushing students to where they feel overwhelmed. Think of it like a target (see Figure 1). In the center of the target is the comfort zone. This is where students are learning content they are already familiar with and are not really being challenged. It might feel comfortable, but there is very little learning going on and certainly no growth. In order to grow students, you have to guide them into the risk zone. There are thousands of strategies to get students into this zone, but no matter which method is used, students should be pushed a little out of their comfort zone, either because the content is something they know nothing about or because they are thinking about it in a different way.

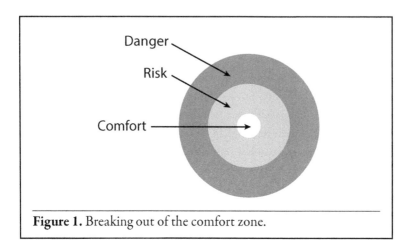

Figure 1. Breaking out of the comfort zone.

This is where students experience the growth and learning we want all students to achieve.

Then, there is the danger zone. This is when a teacher takes a student to a place where he shuts down, either because he is so uncomfortable he is unwilling to learn or the challenge seems like too much of a risk to take. But the challenge is to push students close to the danger zone because the further into risk they are, the more learning takes place. Adding to this challenge is that different students have different target ranges. You can push some students out of their comfort zones, and they adapt. Yet others have a small range, where even a little push might put them in the danger zone. Like any good teacher, one has to be able to differentiate. If you try to teach to one level at one place, or to the middle, as happens in many cases, you will only grow those students and not the high- and low-achieving students. You have to be able to move up and down the spectrum, challenging students who are able and building the stamina of those who might not be ready to be challenged but have the potential.

With all of this uncertainty and lack of a concrete definition, the simplest way to describe underachievement is as *the discrepancy between a child's school performance and his or her ability index as determined by an IQ score.* In other words, if a student tests in the 95th percentile in science, it would be expected that the student's grades in science reflect his or her abilities. This is a comparison between a student's potential and his or her grades.

The good news about underachievement is that it is a behavior, not ability. In other words, underachievers are capable of performing at a high academic level; they just are exhibiting behaviors that are preventing them from doing so. This could be due to discipline issues, a lack of organization, effort, or many other causes that have nothing to do with intelligence. With the right strategies in place, an underachieving student can get back on the right path and reach his potential.

Statistics of Underachievement in the Gifted Population

Just how many gifted students are exhibiting behaviors of under-achievement? You were probably hoping for a chart or graph showing the steady increase of underachieving gifted students over the past 20 years or some other data-based talking point. Unfortunately, because there is much debate about what the definition of *underachieving gifted* is, it is challenging to categorize this group of students. Thankfully, under-achievers in gifted education are sort of like spotting something obscene; there is no clear definition, but you will know them when you see them. And teachers are seeing a lot of them. When an needs assessment was conducted by the National Research Center on the Gifted and Talented, the Number 1 issue concerning the field of gifted education was the underachievement of gifted students (Renzulli, Reid, & Gubbins, 1992).

Anywhere from 10% to 50% of gifted students suffer from under-achievement (Hoffman, Wasson, & Christianson, 1985; Richert, 1991). The varying statistics also depend on gender. In a study by Weiss (1972), 25% of gifted females were considered underachievers, compared to 50% of males. More alarming is that 18% to 25% of students who drop out of high school have been identified as gifted (Center for Comprehensive School Reform and Improvement, 2008). These are students who have the ability to achieve great things, and yet they are not even able to meet the minimum requirements of high school. Somewhere along the way, something got these students off track. Even if that underachieving student is able to get by on his innate ability and graduate, his under-achievement behaviors may follow him to college and beyond. In a study on a group of gifted students (Peterson, 2000), researchers split the students into two categories—high achieving and underachieving. One hundred percent of the high-achieving students went on to a 4-year college, compared to only 87% of the underachievers. Out of those students who went on to a 4-year college, 83% of the high achievers graduated, but nearly half of the underachievers did not (47%). The patterns of behavior that cause underachievement then follow these students into their adult lives. A study of underachieving gifted students 13 years after high school (McCall, Evahn, & Kratzer, 1992) showed they tended to not have the stability in their careers and even their marriages that high achievers did, displaying similar characteristics as they did as students, such as low self-concept, low perception of abilities, lack of persistence, and the inability to accept responsibility for their actions. One of the toughest things is to convince students that these behaviors do not just turn themselves off when they exit the schoolhouse. The learned behaviors carry over into the real world and can affect their success as adults.

Regardless of statistics, there are enough of these students to be concerned, and something needs to be done to reverse the behaviors that cause underachievement.

How Underachievement Can Be Overlooked

The number of underachieving gifted students may be even higher, because in some cases, underachievement can be overlooked. An example would be a gifted student in a regular education classroom. The teacher typically focuses most of her attention on two areas—discipline and low-performing students. She wants to make sure students are not falling too far behind. Thus, if a student is getting B's or even C's, it is not as concerning as a student who is on the verge of failing. If the student getting B's or C's has the ability to be achieving A's, however, he is underachieving. How does one address such a problem when there are students who are performing far worse and the teacher only has so much attention to give? Sometimes a classroom is like a field hospital. There are several people coming in with injuries. The attention is usually given to those who are injured most critically, and the ones who are wounded but will most likely live are kept comfortable but not given the same amount of attention. If a gifted student never raised his hand or participated in class—but also did not stand out by disrupting the learning environment for others—the teacher might simply think the student is doing his best and achieving to the ability he has shown. In reality, this student might only be scratching the surface of his abilities—rather than delving deep into his potential. Because some students are so clever, they learn to play the game of school—you know, the game where you do what you are told, turn in your assignments on time, and appear to be the model student. These students have developed the ability to coast through their classes and take shortcuts that enable them to get the work done, but not achieve at their highest level. They are not identified as underachieving because they are able to operate under the radar, and the teacher may not even be aware that the student is not working to his potential. Some of the actions these students might take include (Post, 2015):

>> taking "easier" classes to avoid more effort;
>> avoiding competitive academic activities, such as the debate team or math contests, to evade potentially envious reactions from peers;
>> refusing to try anything that might lead to failure or rejection, such as auditioning for the lead in the school play;
>> procrastinating until the last minute to see how quickly they can write a paper before a deadline;
>> taking pride in only reading SparkNotes and still getting A's in their AP English class;
>> avoiding opportunities to challenge themselves when given the chance by teachers or assignments; or
>> giving minimal responses to assignments—enough to answer the question but not enough to probe it at a deeper level (para. 4).

Anytime this student can get by on minimal effort, he has, in effect, "outsmarted" the game of school. It might even be something he takes pride in.

Misunderstandings and Myths of Underachievement

Oftentimes, when a student is not working up to his potential, we label him with the L-word—*lazy*. If you looked at the issue through this lens, the student is to blame. This is not always the case. There might be other factors contributing to his behavior. We must be careful not to dismiss the student and instead try to diagnose the cause of the behavior and address it. Many times the cause of the behavior is actually the B-word—*bored*. And why is the student bored? Because the unique needs this gifted student possesses are not being met or even acknowledged. Many times, underachievement is caused by a mismatch between the student and his school environment (as cited in Siegle & McCoach, 2001). Of course, sometimes the student is just being lazy, but it is important to develop strategies to help him be more engaged.

Another misconception often made with gifted students is that they are all motivated by grades. Educators believe that gifted students want to display their intelligence in the form of grades due to their intrinsic love of learning. Although grades motivate some gifted students, grades do not motivate others at all, but their love of learning may manifest in other ways. A student might learn everything he possibly can about a favorite band, analyzing the music, evaluating the changes in styles from album to album, and even creating similar music. He might spend most of his waking moments listening to this music, but this motivation might not translate to the classroom. Or what about the girl who uses her talents to create jewelry, even going so far as to sell it on Etsy and turning a profit? The creative outlet motivates her, as well as the financial benefits of selling the jewelry. It is great this student is learning valuable 21st-century skills that will certainly benefit her in life, but how does that manifest itself on an achievement test?

The motivation for some might involve being socially accepted. Classmates might view being the smartest kid in the class as negative. There is also the added difficulty that some gifted students have in social situations because they relate better to people who think like them, which may not be children their own age. These students may value being "cool" or being liked by others as opposed to being viewed as smart or a "nerd." Because of this, gifted students may mask their high abilities in order to fit in better.

What Can Be Done About Underachievement Amongst Gifted Students?

Just as there is no one type of underachieving student, there is no single way to help these students. There are various strategies that can be used to reverse underachievement. Sometimes combining different strategies might be more effective than a single strategy. And each student is different, so you will have to use different combinations, experimenting to find which one is the most effective.

All of these various strategies typically fall under three categories (Whitmore, 1980):

» **Supportive strategies:** These strategies allow students to feel they are part of a "family," versus the "factory" of school. Such strategies would involve holding class meetings to discuss student concerns, designing lessons based on the needs and interests of students, and allowing students to bypass assignments on subjects in which they have previously shown competency through preassessment.

» **Intrinsic strategies:** How do you get someone who does not care about school to care about school? These strategies incorporate the idea that students' self-concepts as learners are tied closely to their desire to achieve academically. A classroom that invites positive attitudes is likely to encourage achievement. In these classrooms, teachers encourage attempts, not just successes. Students have a place where they can take risks and fail, only to pick themselves up and try again. This is what learning is all about. In addition, teachers put the responsibility of learning on the students, allowing them to give input in creating classroom rules and responsibilities as well as evaluating their own work before receiving a grade from the teacher.

» **Remedial strategies:** Gifted students have skills and content they are deficient in. Teachers who are effective in reversing underachieving behaviors recognize that students are not perfect, even gifted ones. Every child is unique and has specific strengths and weaknesses as well as social, emotional, and intellectual needs. With remedial strategies, students maintain their confidence in academics by being able to excel in their areas of strength and interest. At the same time, there are opportunities provided in specific areas of learning deficiencies. This could include study, test-taking, and note-taking skills.

Each of the strategies presented in this book falls into one of these three categories. One is not better than another. The important aspect is diagnosing what is causing the underachievement of the gifted student so that the proper strategies can be mixed together to be effective.

Conclusion

Gifted underachievers come in all shapes and sizes. Like any group of students, there is no one way to reach them. Different strategies need to be applied to different types of underachievers. The key is first identifying who is gifted in your classroom. Many times teachers are not even aware that a student has been identified gifted in the area they are teaching. With this knowledge should come a different set of expectations. No longer is mastery or proficiency the goal with these students. The goal is to find a way to get them to a higher level, the level they have the potential to achieve. That means developing strategies where the best learning possible takes place. This does not mean giving gifted students more work—it means gifted students need to be challenged, especially in their thinking.

Profiles of Underachievement

If underachieving students all fit the same mold, they would certainly be easier to identify. You could easily keep your eye out for this student and get him the assistance he needs to be successful. There is no one profile for an underachieving student, however. These profiles show the varied ways in which underachievement can manifest.

Profile 1

This student is highly creative. Unfortunately, this creativity clashes with the traditional classroom, where he hates strict, regimented academics. He does love learning, excelling when he finds something that interests him and is given the space to explore it. Unfortunately, the student is not given the opportunity to do this much in school. The teacher gets equally frustrated because she knows this student is very bright but is a nonconformist. He would rather give his opinion on something than a correct answer, which clashes with her style of teaching. He ignores any subject that is not of interest to him, and the teacher has had to ask him to leave the classroom on occasion because his questioning of everything was undermining her authority with the other students.

Who is this student? Scientist Albert Einstein.

Profile 2

This student is a frequent mover between school districts. Because of this, he does not really have any close friends and is treated like an outcast by the other students. He seems to have a poor home life; his father is not on the emergency medical contact list, and his mom's behavior is erratic. Although his grades are very poor, he does seem to have an affinity for English, but rather than reading classics like *The Great Gatsby* or *Of Mice and Men*, he prefers to read comic books. He loves to learn new words, even studying the dictionary at times. If he were asked, he would say that he is smart, but also that he hates school. This student will fail the ninth grade three times and eventually drop out at age 17.

Who is this student? Rapper Eminem.

Profile 3

This is a student who was in gifted programming in elementary school, but the transition to higher grades was more difficult due to many social factors. Throughout his academic career, he has shown a propensity for math and technology, even being put in charge of the school's computer server and running the sound system for many of the school plays. In high school he takes some advanced-level classes but receives average grades. His teachers and parents believe he is capable of much more, but he seems content just getting by. They think his lack of motivation is because he does not want to stand out from the crowd, especially in a school where there are a lot of bullies who prey on differences.

Who is this student? Columbine shooter Dylan Klebold.

Profile 4

This student just has a disdain for school. He consistently scores in the bottom half of his class and is tardy most days. This student has become bored with school, complaining he does not learn anything that is of interest to him. Because of this, he constantly clashes with the authority of the school, causing trouble whenever possible and getting into fights with other students. The only subject he seems to care about is history, which is also the only class he does well in. He can memorize quite well, winning a school contest by memorizing 1,200 lines of a poem. He has interest in being in the military, but his teachers think he is not good enough at math to be successful. He has applied to schools but was placed 390th out of 693 candidates. He also is not very respectful to adults.

Who is this student? Prime Minster Winston Churchill.

Profile 5

This student has been homeschooled for her childhood education. She enjoys fantasy play and creating characters. She also is an excellent reader and good at problem solving, but has difficulty with spelling, math, foreign language, and the mechanics of writing. She often has to recite her answers, and someone else writes them down because her handwriting is so poor. In math, she often forgets numbers, which makes it difficult for her to do even the most rudimentary arithmetic problem. She is eventually diagnosed with a learning disability called dysgraphia, as well as dyslexia, which cause her to have great difficulty with math and writing.

Who is this student? Author Agatha Christie.

In each of these profiles, the cause of underachievement was different. Einstein suffered from boredom, Eminem had a poor home life, Dylan Klebold faced social problems at school, Winston Churchill did not like authority, and Agatha Christie had a learning disability. You would be hard-pressed to find someone who would not proclaim each of these individuals to be gifted. Most of these people went on to become very successful in life despite their early underachievement in school, but how many students who are underachievers do not go on to bigger and better things? How many of them might have developed the latest technological product, written an award-winning film, or come up with a cure to cancer? When you think of the bright minds that have never been completely fulfilled because of suffering from underachievement, it makes one ill. If this book were to help a single student who has fallen into this trap of underachievement, then it will have been a success.

Prototype of an Underachiever

This still does not answer the question: What exactly does an underachiever look like? It would certainly be nice if all underachievers fit the same profile, that they could be spotted easily amongst other students because they wear different colored socks or are identified by the exact same behaviors. We know this is not the case. Just like any other group, there is a lot of diversity amongst underachievers. Part of the reason for this is because different students have different reasons for underachieving. According to Whitmore (1989), there are three broad causes of underachievement:

1. lack of motivation,
2. environments that either do not nurture their gifts or may even discourage high achievement, and
3. a disability that masks the giftedness.

All five of the profiles fit into one of these categories. Because there are many causes of underachievement, it can manifest itself differently. However, there are certain common characteristics that underachieving gifted students possess. Just like symptoms for an illness, some of these might be present, and some of them might not, but if you see enough of the characteristics, you should be able to identify an underachiever. These include:

» low self-esteem,
» negative attitude toward school,
» reluctance to take any risks,
» avoidance of competition,
» lack of perseverance,
» social isolation,
» weaknesses in skill areas and organization,
» lack of goal-directed behavior, and
» being a disruption in class or being resistant to class activities (Baum, Schader, & Owen, 2017; Rimm, 1986; VanTassel-Baska, 1992; Whitmore, 1986).

If we look at Winston Churchill, he suffered from most of these symptoms. He certainly had a negative attitude toward school, lacked perseverance, was weak in many skills and organization, did not possess goal-directed behavior, and was often a disruption in class. Eminem experienced social isolation, had a negative view of school, and was reluctant to take any academic risks.

Sylvia Rimm, in her seminal book *Why Bright Kids Get Poor Grades and What You Can Do About It* (2008), described at great length 15 types of underachievers (see Table 1). You might recognize a lot of students you have among these types. You also might have several components of these types in a single student. You will notice there are two categories of underachievement: There is underachievement that the student can control, and there is underachievement the student cannot control.

As educators, we are often fighting against factors that are out of our control. A teacher can bang his head against the wall trying to get a student with a poor home life to care about her education, but he is dealing with factors that are completely out of his realm of influence. He cannot make this girl's parents care for her, nor can he control the 16 hours she is not in school. When it comes to factors out of our control, we need to try to control the only thing we can— how we treat that student while she is in our classroom.

The Caring Factor

One of the biggest factors to combating underachieving gifted students is caring. Steven Meyers (2009) conducted research on how much it means to students to have a teacher they believe cares about them. He found that "a professor's positive attitude toward students accounted for 58 percent of the variability in the students' motivation, 42 percent of the variability in course appreciation, and 60 percent of students' attitude about the instructor" (p. 206). You can use all of the strategies in this book, but the best way a student who is underachieving is going to perform better is if he thinks that you care. Having someone who shows he or she cares can go a long way with underachievers. Let us go back and look at our five profiles.

> » *Albert Einstein* was mentored by Max Talmey, a medical student who met 10-year old Einstein. He ate lunch weekly with the Einstein family and gave the boy several books about science and philosophy. They interacted for a period of 5 years,

TABLE 1
Rimm's Types of Underachievers and Their Characteristics

Type of Underachiever	Characteristics	Can Control	Cannot Control
Perfectionist Pearl	Afraid to try anything for fear of making a mistake.		✓
Poor Polly	Thrives on the attention she gets from people feeling sorry for her.	✓	
Passive Paul	Lacks motivation.	✓	
Sick Sam	Misses a lot of school or class with "headaches" or "stomachaches."	✓	✓
Taunted Terris	Picked on for being different.		✓
Depressed Donna	Sad and cries a lot and seems tired all of the time.		✓
Torn Tomas	Child of divorce who is being pulled between two homes.		✓
Jock Jack	Focuses more on being a good athlete than being a good student.	✓	
Social Saundra	Cares more about making friends and being social than appearing smart.	✓	
Academic Alice	Was top of her class early in her academic career, but competition of others causes her anxiety, and she feels like a small fish in a large pond.	✓	
Manipulative Maria	Lies to get herself an advantage.	✓	
Creative Chris	Doesn't see the point of school so as a result is a nonconformist.	✓	
Rebellious Rebecca	Discipline problem who doesn't know what she is for but knows what she is against.	✓	

TABLE 1, *Continued.*

Type of Underachiever	Characteristics	Can Control	Cannot Control
Hyperactive Harry	Disorganized student who has difficulty paying attention and keeping focused.		✓
Bully Bob	Quick temper who intimidates fellow students and even adults to get his way.	✓	

Note. Adapted from Rimm, 2008.

which coincided with Einstein underperforming at school because he did not care for the strict rote learning.

» Although *Agatha Christie* grew up in a happy home, schooled by her mother, she did not get the chance to interact with other kids much but did form a friendship with a group of girls with whom she was in a production of a play. This is what caused her to grow to love the theatre and became interested in writing.

» *Dylan Klebold* wrote in his journals that he felt as though no one cared for him other than his parents and his close circle of friends. He suffered from depression and suicidal thoughts that nobody knew about. This lack of care caused much resentment of his classmates, which built up to the Columbine shootings.

» *Eminem* did not have many role models growing up, but one who did show he cared about him was Ronnie Polkinghorn, his mother's half-brother. He introduced Eminem to rap by giving him the *Breakin'* soundtrack with a song featuring Ice-T. They would record rap tapes together that started Eminem down the road to rap stardom.

» *Winston Churchill's* parents were important figures in English society but were neglectful, not spending much time with him as a youth. The person who did was his nanny, Elizabeth Ann Everest, who taught him reading, writing, and arithmetic. She also acted as a close confidant, whom he could go to when he needed to talk to someone. She is often credited with instilling in him the morals that guided him as a leader of his country.

Let us play the "What if?" game. What if these people had not had someone who cared about them enough to encourage them to use their talents? Would they have become the people we know them to be? Would Einstein have studied science if not for the books Talmey exposed him to? Would Christie have had the confidence with her disability to attempt writing had she first not been exposed to it through the theatre? If Eminem's uncle did not give him that rap album, would he have been another high school dropout trying to get by? Would Churchill have been able to lead England through World War II had his nanny not shown she cared? What might have happened differently with Columbine if Dylan Klebold felt as though one of his teachers cared about him? "What ifs" leave one to think about how different these individuals would have ended up had they had or not had someone who cared about them. They also cause one to wonder what young people are currently out there in the world who need someone to show that he or she cares in order to be successful in their endeavors.

How to Spot an Underachiever

The best way to spot an underachiever is to look not at the student but at his behaviors. Table 2 includes revised profiles of the gifted and talented underachiever (Betts & Neihart, 1988). If you can recognize the behaviors of students, you might be able to identify them as underachieving.

Conclusion

In short, there is no easy way to spot an underachieving gifted student. Like most things in life, you have to dig a little bit below the surface in order to find the true picture. It is important when looking for underachievers that you spot the behaviors, not the student. Even the most clean-cut, well-behaved student might not be working to his potential because he does not like to take risks, yet a seemingly unorganized misfit of a student might be doing amazing, mind-blowing learning in his free time. Once you recognize these underachieving gifted students, you can start to use the strategies used throughout the rest of the book.

TABLE 2
Profiles of Gifted and Talented Underachievers

Type of Underachiever	What They Look Like	Behaviors
The Successful	These are students who are motivated and bright, and as a result doing very well in your class. However, they are playing the game of school in order to please the teacher or to be accepted, rather than to develop their high abilities.	• Well-behaved • Conformists • Like structure • Do not like to take risks • Teacher pleasers
The Creative	These students are often frustrated because the school system does not recognize and/or reward their gift of creativity. Instead, they watch as less creative people are acknowledged for following directions and being well behaved. As a result, this student can become frustrated and resentful, leading to misbehavior.	• Can be obstinate and often sarcastic • Might question or challenge authority • Sometimes class clowns • Can be arrogant • Not necessarily popular with peers
The Underground	These students have made a choice to fit in with their peers instead of being academically successful. Because of this, they will not try their best in order to be accepted by these friends.	• May act dumb to fit in • May be insecure • Strong need to belong • Show signs of anxiety • Could feel guilty for masking their gifts
The At-Risk	These students often are resentful of school in general and the adults working there because their needs are not being met. They may physically be in the class, but they are certainly not present.	• Can be depressed and withdrawn • Act defensively • Poor performance • Low self-esteem • Do not care about school

TABLE 2, *Continued.*

Type of Underachiever	What They Look Like	Behaviors
The Twice-Exceptional	These students are gifted but also have some sort of disability, whether physical, emotional, or learning. More focus may be on the disability rather than the gift.	• Display disruptive behavior • Act frustrated • Confused about their gifts • Don't like when their disabilities are focused on
The Autonomous Learner	These students know how to play the game of school and gets good grades as a result. However, they do not value school as the place to learn. They have their own interests, which they explore at great length, but are not always synonymous with what school wants them to learn.	• Show tolerance and respect for others • Use system to succeed • Independent • Self-directed • Respected and liked by teachers and peers

Note. Adapted from "Profiles of the Gifted and Talented" by G. Betts and M. Neihart, 1988, *Gifted Child Quarterly, 23,* pp. 250–251.

Part II

10 CAUSES OF UNDERACHIEVEMENT AND PRACTICAL SOLUTIONS

Cause 1

BOREDOM

When you were a child, do you remember how much you loved school? You were eager to go, you had nothing but good things to say, and when weekends came it was a bit of a disappointment. Then, something happened. There was a tipping point, maybe around middle school, when school transformed from something that you could not wait to do, to something you had to do. It became like a job, dreading Mondays and awaiting Fridays. What happened between the first and latter years? Why do a majority of students come to dread going to school—even though it is the place that houses all of their friends? The major culprit for this switch is boredom.

How did things go so wrong so fast? Why did schools change from the place where everything was new and exciting, to the place where you had to bear down and suffer through so that you could go on and do things you would rather do? A lot of it has to do with how schools are set up in general. In elementary schools, one teacher is typically in charge of 25 students. As any elementary teacher will tell you, you have to keep the students busy; otherwise they will begin to get antsy. So, elementary teachers have a lot of tricks up their sleeves, rotating students through centers, hands-on activities, etc. They keep them out of trouble by keeping them busy. Middle schools and high schools tend to turn to structure in order to maintain order. This means keeping students in perfectly formed rows, and putting the teacher at the front of the classroom, disseminating information while students passively learn. Putting them in collaborative groups or having them in centers might make for a noisy class. Controlling the room cuts down on behavior issues. Of course, this makes students much more inactive, and this is when boredom can begin.

There is also more of a personal connection in an elementary school because teachers usually have students all day, all year. There is time to cultivate relationships, and students, especially compliant ones, want to please their teacher. On the other hand, a high school teacher could have five classes of 25, and only for 45 minutes to an hour a day. Just getting to know students' names is enough of a challenge, much less getting to know each of them. Amazingly, many high school teachers excel at this, although the degree of difficulty is much higher than that of an elementary teacher.

The other issue with the later grades, and with gifted students especially, is that the gap between student knowledge and skill can widen over time. In other words, in elementary school, a gifted student might be a little ahead of his fellow students, familiar with higher level vocabulary, and able to process content a little faster. Because that student gets a little more ahead each year, by the time he reaches middle or high school, he is way ahead of classmates. As the teacher teaches to the pace of the typical student, this means the gifted students are going at a slow pace and covering content they may already be familiar with. What could be more boring than learning the basics about something you already know?

The overreliance on teacher-led learning and lack of a connection with the teacher at the higher levels of education both combine, causing boredom. The abilities of the gifted student only accentuate this boredom, which is a major cause of underachievement amongst gifted students.

When Students Have to Stay With the Class

Teachers often feel they need to keep everybody in the class moving at the same pace. The traditional classroom has a traditional setup. Students are seated in desks in rows facing the front of the classroom, where the teacher dispenses information like the sage on the stage. There is a central focus on memorization of facts and application of content.

What throws a wrench in this traditional structure is the student who is moving at a quicker pace than a majority of the class. In many cases, the response to this fast-paced learner is one of two things: (1) Have the student slow down and stay with the class, or (2) if the student finishes early, have her complete extra work that addresses more of what she has already been doing. It will not take a gifted student long to figure out that if she gets her work done too fast, it will just result in more work, which takes away the advantage of finishing early. Then, the student learns to pace herself so that she gets her work done but never gets too far ahead of the rest of the class. This slow pace can be extremely boring, just as the fast pace for someone with a learning disability can be too challenging.

Tracking has become a bad word in education, and yet that is exactly what we are doing by placing students into classes based on age. By putting students in a specific grade, we are lumping a group of students together based only on their birthdate. Anyone who has spent any amount of time in education knows that you can have 15-year-old students you can have an adult conversation with and 15-year-old students who still believe in Santa Claus. And yet we are putting these vastly different children in the same classroom and expecting them to achieve at the exact same level. This is not realistic, but it is the structure education has chosen to adopt. If we were setting up our ideal educational system, students would take subjects that were more ability-appropriate than age-appropriate. That would mean having students of various ages taking an algebra class or a low-level high school student taking classes with middle school children. We know that this is next to impossible in our current configuration because students are separated into buildings by age—elementary, middle, high, and even junior high schools.

An accomplished teacher figures out how to let students move at the pace that best suits them so that they do not become bored or overwhelmed. This is easier said than done. It requires more work from the teacher. This is what differentiation is, and it looks very different than the traditional classroom. You may have 30 students in your classroom with 17 working on one thing, 10 working on something a little less challenging, and 3 students working at greater depth than the rest. This is difficult to plan and to manage, but it can be done. The challenge is finding all of the levels of differentiation. In other words, juggling two different levels would be difficult enough, but depending on your class, you might need five or six different levels. By doing this, the pace is not determined by the teacher but instead by the students.

When Boredom Grows

Underachievement usually begins when a student no longer feels challenged by school. In the early years of school, everything is so new, and students know so little that they can have a teacher who does not challenge them and still be challenged by the content. When students get older and get to know more, it becomes more obvious to them that they are not being challenged. If students go 2 or 3 years without any teachers to challenge them, then they might fall into the rut of under-achievement. This is why underachievement rears its ugly head mostly in middle and high school. The school is not keeping up with the student's ability, so instead there is a lot of repetition and passive learning. If students are given work to supplement their ability, it is just more of the same. And, of course, the worst thing a teacher can do is have a gifted student tutor a struggling student. This does not actually benefit the gifted student. He still is dealing with content on a lower level and has to go even lower to make it accessible to the struggling student. If you want to enrich the gifted student, you should go in the other direction, finding a mentor who is an expert in the subject and can supplement what the gifted student is learning.

Not only does boredom lead to underachievement, it can lead to behavior problems as well. There is a reason for the saying, "Idle hands are the devil's handiwork." When gifted students become bored they find other things to do—some productive, some not so productive. This might be talking to a fellow classmate, not working on the work they are supposed to, and instead doing something else or outwardly chal-lenging the teacher. It can eventually lead to even more serious offenses, such as tardiness, fights with other students, or truancy. Many of these students would not be behavior problems if only they were engaged in the class. These students might be behavior problems in classes they are not interested in but ideal students in those classes they are interested in.

According to Michael Linsin (2012), there are several things that can lead to student boredom:

1. *Sitting too long*: No one likes to sit all day being talked at. This might seem like excellent training for the adult world of sitting in long, boring meetings, but if students are made to sit too long, they will become unengaged. Make sure you pay attention to student body language and get them moving if a majority becomes fidgety.

2. *Talking too much*: To quote Run-D.M.C., "You talk too much, you never shut up." Human beings have an attention span that, even for a person who can concentrate very well, lasts no more than 20 minutes. Those who are not giving that effort might only last 10 minutes or even 5. Students need to be moving, involved, and engaged. Talking at them for an hour is not going to accomplish this.

3. *Making the simple complex*: There is a difference between a complex problem and a problem that requires a student to think at a higher level. Many teachers do not understand how to increase the level of thinking without making the problem complex. They take it to mean that they need to make their instruction more difficult. And yet some of the most thought-provoking questions can be so simple. An example of a higher level question: *What is your favorite color and why?* The justification of the choice is in the evaluation aspect of Bloom's taxonomy (see p. 153 for more information about this concept). Teachers need to be teaching students to critically think using this simple questioning.

4. *Making the interesting, uninteresting*: This all comes down to delivery. If you deliver even the most interesting topic in a method that has students sitting and listening, it will quickly become uninteresting. At the same time, you can take something seemingly uninteresting and make it interesting by engaging students and connecting it to the real world. If you

the teacher are not interested in the topic, it will be very difficult for students to become interested.

5. *Directing too much, observing too little*: Teachers sometimes feel the need to act as cruise director. Some run the show and never sit back and watch students learn for themselves. You should never be working harder than your students. They should be doing the bulk of the work with you guiding from the side. As Sherlock Holmes was known to say, "You see, but you do not observe. The distinction is clear."

6. *Leading a slow, sloppy, slipshod pace*: There are a variety of students in the classroom. You may have special education students who need to move at a slower pace, regular students who move at a traditional pace, and gifted students who move at an advanced pace. If you are not skilled at differentiation, you typically teach to the middle. You leave yourself enough space to work with those who may fall behind, but the gifted students have to put on the brakes. If they get too far ahead, the rest of the class will never catch up. This slow, crawling pace often causes gifted students to become bored.

7. *Failing to adjust*: Any teacher worth her salt must be skilled at adjusting. This means pace, content, rigor, etc. If even the best teacher keeps doing the same thing over and over without adjusting, students could easily become bored.

The key is to find teaching strategies that avoid these causes of boredom. Although there are many strategies a teacher can use to combat boredom in the classroom, the following may solve many of the aforementioned causes.

Practical Solutions

Strategy 1: Preassessment

Just how much does a student know about a given topic? There are times we just assume students do not know anything. Thus, when we begin to teach a topic, we start at the very beginning. There may be some students who benefit from this. There are others who will already know the basics and will be bored having to start at the beginning. What if, before a unit begins, you give a preassessment to see how much students already know? Many teachers do this. But what do teachers do with that information? Unfortunately, if students show mastery of the content, they are often still made to go through the unit at the same pace as everyone else.

The days of all students being treated the same are long gone. We know through research and observation that students are different from one another, and thus their education should reflect this. If you have a student who is learning disabled, you should teach that student very differently than a typical student. In fact, laws require accommodations for these students. Unfortunately, there is no such law in the gifted realm. Because of this, gifted students often get lost in the shuffle. They are able to keep up with the class, so teachers assume they are fine when in fact they could be moving even quicker or going more in depth.

If a student takes a preassessment and shows he has mastery of the content, what if you give him credit for that without him having to go through the material at the rest of the class's pace? Can the preassessment act as the proof that this student understands the content? Of course, the logical question is: What does that student do while the rest of the class learns the regular content? This is where you have the opportunity to really challenge a gifted student. You can have the student create an independent study either based on the content you are covering, allowing the student to explore it more in depth, or you can have him choose an independent study based on something he wants to learn about related to the subject area. You can even create a contract with the student (see Figure 2).

You can meet with the student periodically to make sure he is on track to finish the project. Other than that, you can stay out of the student's way and make sure he has the resources he needs to work on his independent study. By doing this, you are combating many of the causes of boredom because independent study allows students to go in depth on a topic and manage their own pace.

Project Contract

Student Name: _____

Project Name: _____

Estimated Time of Project:_____
(include calendar)

Power Standard(s) Covered: _____

Other Standards Covered: _____

_____

_____

Skills Learned:

- _____
- _____
- _____

Overall Goal of Project: _____

_____

_____

Product of Project: _____

_____

_____

Headings for Rubric Evaluation: _____

_____

_____

(include rubric)

Student Signature: _____

Teacher's Signature: _____

Parent(s) Signature:_____

Figure 2. Project contract. From *Project-Based Learning for Gifted Students: A Handbook for the 21st-Century Classroom* (p. 17), by T. Stanley, 2012, New York, NY: Routledge Copyright Copyright 2012 by Taylor & Francis. Reprinted with permission.

In addition to preventing boredom, there are educational advantages to students working independently (DeNeen, 2013). Students:

1. learn how to learn,
2. focus on the process and not just the goal,
3. learn at their level of intelligence,
4. learn time management and other life skills,
5. experience passion and curiosity that cement their learning,
6. experience internal satisfaction,
7. become more aware of their own strengths and weaknesses,
8. learn how to educate others,
9. can self-critique more effectively, and
10. learn resourcefulness.

Using preassessments to allow students to bypass content they already know and instead working on something of their own creation will motivate them much more.

Strategy 2: Project-Based Learning

Project-based learning (PBL) is a strategy of teaching that provides many advantages, including (Stanley, 2012):

» allowing more creativity,
» differentiation of varying ability levels,
» creating a passion for learning, and
» motivating underachieving gifted students (p. vii).

PBL involves students being given a task to accomplish, usually addressing an essential question the teacher has provided or, even better, one that the teacher and students have created together. Students are either asked to create a product to demonstrate mastery of this concept or are allowed to choose a product they feel will do this. PBL is typically long-term, spanning over weeks rather than just a single day. It is also usually done in groups, which allows for collaboration, although projects can be completed individually.

The most effective aspect of PBL, when it comes to addressing the boredom of underachieving gifted students, is that it naturally differentiates. If a student comes into the project knowing a lot of information about the content, then she can start her project at that point and go as deep as she likes. There is no ceiling on a project because the product allows for a lot of different possibilities to demonstrate mastery. There is also no one correct answer. There are several possibilities because the essential question is open-ended. Figure 3 is an example of a project.

You could give this project to 25 different students and get 25 very different models at 25 different levels of understanding. There would be some who get a basic understanding of the content, but someone else might be breaking new ground. They would all be answering the essential questions, some in more depth than others. This organic differentiation allows you to juggle the various levels of ability, because the students themselves determine how deep they are going to go. You may need to provide some encouragement and coaching, especially for those underachieving gifted students who have gotten used to doing the bare minimum. But by giving them choice and allowing for more creativity, bored students might become engaged in learning.

Strategy 3: Alternative Assessments

We live in an educational world of high-stakes testing. Nearly every state has an achievement test that measures student progress over the course of the year. These assessments are primarily made up of multiple-choice questions, and to prepare students, we expose them to this type of assessment. Unfortunately, we sometimes take it too far, and every assessment becomes a pencil-to-paper test. Since you have been out of school, how many pencil-to-paper tests have you had to take? Not many. Most assessments in your adult life are going to be performance-based. These are assessments where instead of indicating a correct or incorrect answer, you are producing a product of some sort.

Some examples of performance-based assessment include (Stanley, 2014):
» oral presentations,
» debates/speeches,
» role-playing,
» group discussions,

Paper: It's Not Just for Writing

Brief Description

Origami is the art of paper design through folding. It involves angles both in the model folded as well as in the unfolded paper. Learn how math and origami are linked and try some of the patterns.

Product

You will create origami animals and research those animals. You will make several of these, either creating a farm, zoo, jungle, or other habitat with many animals. You will also try to invent your own creation in origami paper design, explaining how it is created mathematically.

Content Areas

English/Science/Math

Essential Questions

- How do you locate important details about a topic using different sources of information including books and online resources?
- How do animals fit together in a habitat?
- How does origami use math in order to accomplish the shapes it does?

Inspiration Starting Point

Read "Origami & Math" (available at http://www.paperfolding.com/math)

Estimated Time of Project

2 weeks

Suggested Materials

- Paper
- Patterns for origami (available at http://www.paperfolding.com)

Figure 3. An example of project-based learning.

> » interviews,
> » portfolios,
> » exhibitions,
> » essays,
> » research papers, and
> » journals/student logs. (p. 43)

Using performance-based assessments allows you to engage under-achievers in a way that traditional testing does not. Performance-based assessments tend to be more hands-on, allow for greater use of creativity, and encourage valuable 21st-century survival skills that will benefit students later in life. The challenge in using performance-based assessments is grading them because they can be subjective, given that there is not just one correct answer. How does a teacher ensure that she is properly measuring whether the student has learned the content or not? The best way to do this is through a well-written rubric. Figure 4 is an example of what a rubric evaluating an oral presentation would look like.

This particular rubric breaks down the performance into two parts—the content of the presentation and the professionalism of the presentation. The essential question is addressed by the content, and the professionalism of the presentation is a 21st-century skill, as is the group work aspect, which measures the effectiveness of the collaboration. These 21st-century skills could not be captured on a multiple-choice test, but with an effective rubric, they can be properly measured.

To make a final case for performance-based assessment, if you think back to the moments in school that you remember, you are probably not thinking about the time you bubbled in a particular letter on a test or when a teacher was lecturing *at* you. Performance-based assessments, such as building an invention, performing a scene from a book, or giving a presentation to the class, are probably what stand out the most. Why would you not want to provide students with these memorable moments that will elicit an enduring understanding? These types of assessments will engage the students and make it more difficult to become bored.

Rubric for Discovery Unit

	Content	Presentation	Group Work
Excellent	• Students teach the information in the standard in depth, providing a deeper understanding than needed. • Students are clear in their teaching of the content, providing examples and detail to help with understanding. • The questions the group provides capture the standard and all aspects of it.	• Student presentation is well-organized, with everyone sure of his or her role and what is being taught. • Visuals and handouts that the group uses bring meaning to the presentation and are well-explained. • Students are confident in their speaking ability and are easily heard by the audience.	• Students work well with one another, listening to everyone's ideas and allowing all to contribute. • Students are on task as a group, working with focus and getting tasks done on time. • Students do a good job of incorporating everyone's strengths into the design of the presentation.
Good	• Students teach the information in the standard at a surface level, providing the basics but not getting a deeper understanding.	• Student presentation is organized, but some group members are not sure of their roles, or there is a moment of confusion.	• Students work well with one another but don't always listen to each other's ideas and allow everyone to contribute.

Figure 4. Sample performance-based assessment rubric.

	Content	Presentation	Group Work
Good, *continued.*	• Students provide examples and detail to help with understanding but need more to help with clarity. • The questions the group provides capture the standard but not all aspects of it.	• Visuals and handouts the group uses bring a basic understanding, but need to be explained better for deeper meaning. • Students are confident in their speaking ability and are easily heard by the audience most of the time, but mumble or are unclear at times.	• Students are on task as a group, working with focus and getting tasks done, but occasionally get sidetracked. • Students do a good job of incorporating everyone's strengths into the design of the presentation most of the time, but not always.
Needs Improvement	• Students do not teach the information in the standard, missing the concept they are supposed to address. • Students are not clear in their teaching of the content, causing confusion by not providing examples and detail to help with understanding. • The questions the group provides do not capture the standard and/or are off topic.	• Student presentation is not well organized, with group members often unsure of their role and what is being taught. • Visuals and handouts the group uses do not bring meaning to the presentation and seem off topic. • Students are not confident in their speaking ability, making them hard to be heard by the audience.	• Students do not work well with one another, not listening to everyone's ideas and allowing all to contribute. • Students are not on task as a group, lacking focus and not getting tasks done on time. • Students do not adequately incorporate everyone's strengths into the presentation, leaving group members out.

Figure 4. *Continued.*

Conclusion

Combating boredom is something teachers struggle with on a daily basis. Today, when students have much shorter attention spans and their ability to delay gratification is nearly nonexistent, it is even more of a challenge. Of course, it is not our job to entertain the students, but it is our job to engage them in learning. Using one of these strategies with your gifted underachievers to prevent their boredom does not guarantee success, but it would make your classroom more engaging and challenge students.

If you would like to read more in depth about one of these strategies or topics, a good resource is *Project-Based Learning for Gifted Students: A Handbook for the 21st-Century Classroom* by Todd Stanley, or *Performance-Based Assessment for 21st-Century Skills* by Todd Stanley.

Cause 2

SOCIAL-EMOTIONAL NEEDS

Along with their academic needs, just as important, if not more important, are the social-emotional needs of gifted children. Many gifted students, in addition to having a heightened sense of thinking, have a heightened sense of emotion. Something that might seem innocuous to someone else might upset this gifted student. For example, if students are told to get in line by alphabetical order and two students are standing in the wrong place, a gifted student might take exception to this and want the problem to be fixed, while other students do not pay it any attention. Especially prevalent amongst gifted students is a strong sense of fairness. If something appears unfair, a gifted student is going to have a tougher time accepting it than other students might.

Because these social-emotional needs can be intense, addressing them is important. If they are not addressed, they can often come into conflict with the intellectual abilities of a gifted child and lead to under-achievement. For example, there are some gifted students who have great difficulty collaborating with others. This may be because they feel the group is not listening to them, it might be that they perceive they are doing more work than everyone else, or it may be that they feel they are being treated in an unfair manner. This perceived feeling of unfairness might cause the student to shut down and not work with the group any longer. It can appear to the teacher that the student is being belligerent, but in that child's mind, he is just refusing to continue to contribute to a situation that is not fair to him.

Some common social-emotional needs of gifted children are:

- » social acceptance,
- » intensity,
- » need for precision,
- » overexcitabilities,
- » acute self-awareness,
- » nonconformity,
- » questioning of authority, and
- » sensitivity to global problems.

You might look at this list and think: Are these not issues for most children? The answer, of course, is yes, but with many gifted children, the issues are magnified.

Consider sensitivity to global problems. Many students, even high school students, are not very globally aware. They see the world only 5 feet in front of them and believe the biggest problems exist within this vacuum. There are some gifted children who worry excessively about large world problems, such as hunger, war, global warming, and homelessness. They actually stay up late at night, unable to get to sleep because they are concerned with something occurring on the other side of the planet. Silverman (2011) stated, "I have found that the higher the child's IQ, the earlier moral concerns develop and the more profound effect they have on the child" (para. 8). Because it takes maturity and resources before the child can do anything about the problem, he is simply left to worry about it. This goes back to gifted students' strong sense of fairness, which manifests itself into a moral sensitivity about injustices not only specific to them, but also to the world. It is not fair that girls in Africa cannot get an education or that Northern hairy-nosed wombats are becoming endangered in Australia.

Table 3 is a list of the social-emotional attributes and potential problems amongst gifted students.

Gifted children have quirks. These are simply part of the gifted students' personalities. Some interpret these quirks as negative and want to change them. It is the attempt to change these that causes gifted students to question authority. According to the National Association for Gifted Children (NAGC, n.d.b), you need to keep in mind when working with gifted students that:

TABLE 3

Social-Emotional Issues of Gifted Students

Attribute	Potential Problem When Attribute is Not Supported or Developed
High performance standards	Unhealthy perfectionism Severe procrastination Significant mood swings
Internal motivation	Anxiety Poor resiliency
Emotional intensity	Easily emotionally hurt by others Overly self-critical
Empathy	Can trigger emotional intensity
Moral maturity	Rigid sense of justice Difficulties with peer interactions
Self-actualization	Existential depression at a very young age
Resiliency	Poor resources to combat anxiety and/or emotional distress

Note. Adapted from *Understanding the Social and Emotional Lives of Gifted Students* (p. 55), by T. P. Hébert, 2011, New York, NY: Routledge Copyright 2011 by Taylor & Francis. Adapted with permission.

» giftedness can lead to the masking and misunderstanding of underlying problems;

» not all gifted children are alike, as each has a unique social-emotional profile;

» there is no definitive strategy for maintaining a child's emotional equilibrium;

» parents need to model balance and set the tone to reduce stress and anxiety in their child's life; and

» gifted children can and should be taught tools for dealing with the ebb and flow of life (para. 3).

Understanding these social-emotional needs can go a long way in getting an underachieving gifted student to begin to achieve.

When Gifted Students Lack Impulse Control

Because facts can come quickly to gifted students, they develop a habit of blurting out an answer before anyone else has had the opportunity to process the question in an effort to show others how much they know. Teachers and other students can view this as a lack of discipline. There is supposed to be order in a classroom. Students are supposed to raise their hand before answering a question and then wait to be called on. Anything other than this can be perceived as a behavior issue. But that is just it—it is a perception. The student is not blurting out an answer in order to defy authority. He has something to share that he believes will benefit everyone else.

Sometimes this lack of impulse control leads to a questioning of authority. Some students may do this because they have a lack of respect for adults, they come from a home where talking back is common, or the teacher consistently gets them in trouble and it has turned into a power struggle. For gifted children, questioning of authority more than likely stems from their innate curiosity. They are not questioning authority because they do not want to do what is being asked of them. They question authority because they believe the teacher is wrong. If a teacher is talking about the layers of the Earth and mixes up the mantle and the crust, the gifted student might raise his hand and point out, "Hey, you're wrong." Some teachers will chalk this up to trying to embarrass them and defying authority, but the student is merely trying to make sure the class has the correct answer. Or there might be a student who questions a teacher's interpretation of a poem because she thinks it might be representing something else. There will be times when a gifted student will know more about a topic than the teacher. This disrupts the notion that the teacher is the expert. Some teachers do not like being questioned or see it as disrespect. Some gifted students do come across as pompous or know-it-alls, so the teacher does not see the questioning as someone who is being curious. She sees it as someone who is challenging her.

When Gifted Students Demonstrate Low Frustration Tolerance

In some ways, there is a certain level of arrogance many gifted students possess. After having teachers and parents for years telling them how smart they are, they come to believe it. That means that others are not as intelligent as them. Because they think they are better than others, many gifted students do not suffer fools gladly. In other words, if someone they deem as less intelligent than them is trying to put forth an idea, the gifted student is not going to be as willing to listen. There needs to be a distinction made between *better at* and *better than*. A gifted student may be better at certain academics. It does not mean he is better than other students. But gifted students can easily become frustrated by classmates who do not understand content as fast as they do or who offer ideas they see as inferior.

This also applies to collaboration. There are some gifted students who just do not collaborate with others very well. Their know-it-all attitude is off-putting to the other group members, and their need to control the group because they think their ideas are better is a source of frustration if the group does not follow their decisions. They hold everyone in the group to impossibly high standards (Silverman, 2007). It makes it difficult for them to work with others and causes frustration because everyone is not performing like they are.

Another source of frustration can be the teacher. Gifted students are sometimes smarter than the people who are teaching them. They come to resent the fact that this person who is less intelligent than them is the one who is trying to teach them and evaluating their progress. They do not defy authority so much as lack respect for it. This can also be a place where the questioning of authority rears its ugly head. Sometimes questioning is intellectual curiosity, and sometimes it is truly a challenge of the teacher because the student thinks he knows better.

A final source of frustration can come at the expense of school itself. If the student is given a lot of repetitive work that she already knows, she will begin to become frustrated by school and shut down, either doing the work in a haphazard manner with little regard to quality, or simply choosing not to do it at all. If this develops early in a child and

49

unless there is a really engaging teacher in later years, she will develop a resentment of school no matter who is teaching. School becomes labeled as a source of frustration, and anything that happens there just becomes more fodder to add to the narrative: School does not teach her the things she wants to know. This, of course, leads to underachievement.

When Gifted Students Are Unwilling to Take Risks

Because gifted students tend to be more knowledgeable than their peers, they develop a reputation for always having the correct answer. This reputation can stay with them and lead to the expectation that this student will always have the answer. That becomes a problem when the student does not have the answers that once came so quickly. If there is any fear his response will be incorrect, the gifted student will not attempt the answer in a public setting because he wants to preserve his reputation of having the correct answers.

As educators, we know that making mistakes is part of the learning process. So what happens to a student who does not want to make any mistakes for fear she will look incompetent? She is going to be denied this process of the learning. Part of this process is also about taking risks, such as trying something you are not quite sure about to see if it will work (revisit Figure 1 on p. 10). In an ideal situation, you want students to be in the risk zone of this target of learning. That is where the most learning is going to take place. If the gifted student is reluctant to take any risks because he sees them as dangers, however, his learning target will look like Figure 5.

The student does not want to wander outside of the comfort zone because he sees everything else as danger. The major problem: If he is in a comfort zone and knows everything that is being covered, nothing new is being learned. There is a reason we call them challenge programs. Students are supposed to be challenged, but there are some gifted students who consider taking a risk a danger. Because of this unwillingness to take risks, this student just stays in the comfort zone and does not grow as a learner.

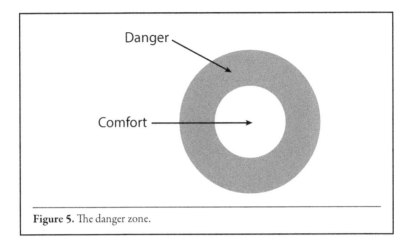

Figure 5. The danger zone.

These social-emotional needs can impede the academic progress of a gifted student if they become too intense. A teacher who is aware of the social-emotional needs of his gifted students and understands their quirks can go a long way toward the students feeling accepted and not allowing social-emotional problems to get in the way of their academic progress.

Practical Solutions

Strategy 1: Allow Students to Challenge the Teacher

Some gifted students like to challenge the teacher. Let them. Make it part of the culture of your classroom. Students should know it is all right to challenge the teacher as long as it is in a positive and productive manner. In order for this to happen, you have to create opportunities where students can challenge you. This way, when they have something challenging they want to say to the teacher, they know it is a safe place to do so. One way you can do this is by handing out written assignments that have a mistake in them. The mistake can be a misspelled word or bad grammar, a math problem that is not set up correctly, or stating a fact incorrectly. Whatever you choose, challenge students to challenge you by finding the mistake.

It could look something like this:

There is a typo in the following parent letter. The first student who discovers it and provides the correction gets a piece of candy:

Dear Ivy Program Parent:

The Ivy Program is taking our first field trip of the year. The field trip will be on Wednesday, December 18. A bus will be coming around to each building and picking up students between 9:30 and 10:00. We will be traveling to the Museum of Art. It opens at 10:00. For the first part of the day, we will be taking part in the Look, Think, Discover Tour arranged at the museum. Their will be docents present to guide students through the exhibit. The second half of the day will involve students exploring the museum, finding a specific piece of art they would like to write a critique on.

In this case, the students would have to read through the letter and figure out that the incorrect version of *their* was used instead of the appropriate *there*.

Or consider something like this:

How much can an elephant eat? Somewhere in this list of facts there is something wrong. Research and figure out which fact is incorrect, and correct it before answering the problem.

An elephant eats a lot of food in the course of a day. See if you can figure out just how much.

1. On average, an adult elephant will eat 300 pounds of food in a single day. How many kilograms of food would this be (1 kilogram = 2.7 pounds)?

2. Elephants are grazing animals, which means instead of eating a few large meals a day like humans, they are feeding and nibbling the entire day. An elephant can spend 20 hours a day feeding. How many pounds of food do they average in an hour?

3. Elephants live to be 70 years old. How many pounds of food would they consume in their lifetime?
4. Around 45% of an elephant's diet is grass. How many pounds of grass would that be in a day?
5. Elephants also need to drink a lot of water. For every gallon of water they drink, they eat 6 pounds of food. How many gallons of water would they drink in a day?

Students would have to look through the facts and determine which ones might not be correct (they would learn through research that 1 kilogram actually equals 2.2 pounds).

Another way to allow students to challenge you is to take part in discussion or debate that allows the students to argue with you in a constructive manner. For example, in science class you are debating which is better, paper or plastic. You have taken the side of plastic and have asked a student to argue the side of paper. You are allowing the student to challenge your opinion in a constructive manner. Or, if you are talking about a piece of literature, there might be a discussion over the intent of a character. You might even play devil's advocate to add fuel to the discussion and get students to a place where they feel comfortable challenging you.

A final way to allow students to challenge you is to allow them to make a case for their grade. Typically, (1) students work on an assignment, (2) the teacher grades it, and (3) when the teacher gives the grade back, the student looks at it and accepts it. There may be an occasional grade grubber seeking an extra point or two, but there is usually no room for discussion about the grade that was assigned. What if you gave students the chance to make a case for their grade? This would not involve them trying to convince you to assign them a different grade. Instead, this would involve sitting down and conferencing with students using a rubric, where they would place themselves in various categories and justify why. You might use a rubric like Figure 6, an example of a group presentation rubric.

A student would then have to decide which level she falls into under each category, justifying her answer by citing examples from her performance and how they match up with the descriptors. Any arguments

Presentation Rubric

Overall	Content	Presentation	Product
Excellent	• Includes many details and examples to defend choices. • Provides clear evidence that answers the learning outcomes on the students' contracts. • Spends more time answering the higher level thinking outcomes than the ones that can be answered with facts they looked up.	• Speakers present clearly and consistently throughout, and do not read to audience. • Everyone is clear on what his or her role is, and transitions between learning are smooth. • Presentation is organized in a professional manner, making it easy to follow what is being discussed.	• Product looks professional, like something that would be used by a teacher. • Clearly adds to the content of the presentation through the use of visuals, demonstrations, or simulations. • Product is easy for people to view and/or understand.
Good	• Includes details and examples to defend choices but is missing them in a few places where it would make the defense clearer.	• Speakers present clearly most times, and read to audience only occasionally. • Most everyone is clear on what his or her role is, but there are some transitions between learning outcomes that could be smoother.	• Product looks somewhat professional, like a good-quality school project.

Figure 6. Sample group presentation rubric.

Overall	Content	Presentation	Product
Good, *continued.*	• Provides evidence that answers most of the learning outcomes students have created on their contracts, but a couple are not as clear as they could be or need more evidence.	• Presentation is organized, making it easy to follow what is being discussed, but it is not as professional as it could be.	• Adds to the content of the presentation through the use of visuals, demonstrations, or simulations, but there are opportunities where more could have been done.
Needs Improvement	• Includes few or no details and examples to defend choices. • Does not provide much evidence that answers the learning outcomes students have created on their contracts. Instead, makes blanket statements that are not backed up.	• Speakers do not present clearly, often reading to the audience. • Some are not clear on what their role is, and transitions between learning outcomes are cumbersome. • Presentation is not organized, making it difficult to follow what is being discussed at any given time.	• Display does not look professional, and looks like something an elementary student would make. • Does not add to the content of the presentation through the use of visual, demonstrations, or simulations. • Product is not easy for people to view/hear, leaving many details out or unclear.

Figure 6. *Continued.*

55

she makes need to be based on the rubric. For instance, if the student places herself in the "good" level in the "presentation" category, she would have to make a case for how the presentation was organized but not as professional as could be, and admit to mistakes in consistency of her speaking and transitions. By grading in this manner, students will feel they had some sort of say in their grade because they were a part of the process.

Challenging the teacher does not work if sometimes you let students challenge you and other times you forbid it. You might fear that you are opening up a can of worms by allowing students to challenge you. The students might ask why they have to learn about something. Of course, if you have trouble justifying why you are asking them to do a particular activity, should you be having them do it? By controlling and allowing for challenging, you do not create a power struggle. Instead, you create an environment where students are comfortable challenging their teacher without resorting to talking back or becoming discipline problems.

Strategy 2: Advisory Groups

Sometimes gifted students just need someone to listen to them. This might be a peer, a family member, or even a teacher. One way you can facilitate this listening is to arrange for advisory groups. This involves gathering a group of gifted students and letting them talk about things that are on their minds. The topics could be as simple as worrying about an upcoming test, or as serious as depression. You would be responsible for providing the space, giving structure to the conversation, and monitoring progress, but you have to be careful that you do not dominate the conversation or prevent the free flow of ideas and thoughts.

In 10th grade, for example, you might identify a cluster of 15 gifted students and invite them to be part of the group, making very clear its purpose. You arrange a time, maybe during their study period, when other students are receiving intervention, or during the latter half of their lunch. You also arrange a space in your classroom or a conference room, but it needs to be somewhere you can close the door and other students and teachers are not going to come in and interrupt. Students sit at desks or chairs you have arranged in a circle. On each desk is an index card. You ask each student to write something that is bothering him or her about school. You can provide a couple of examples, such as "Too much homework in chemistry class is stressing me out," "My geometry teacher doesn't seem to like me," or "I'm worried about getting into college." Collect the cards and read them aloud, not indicating who wrote each, but asking for some feedback on each issue. Like kernels snapping into white, fluffy pieces of popcorn, the conversation might start slowly at first, but then it will pick up steam and begin to pop. Your role is to maintain the momentum of the discussion so it has enough time to grow and take off. Once this happens, the discussion will take on a life of its own, and you can sit back and watch as students resolve their own problems, knowing they are being listened to.

Be sure to set norms for how students behave in the group. These should be established together. You can give students 5–7 sticky notes and provide them with the following prompt: *What do you need in order to be successful in this group?* Have students write one need per sticky note. After giving them some time to do this, invite them up to the whiteboard or a piece of butcher paper hanging on the wall and have them cluster their sticky notes with other students' similar norms. If eight people had something about being respectful, group those sticky notes together. Or maybe half of the group thought it was important to participate. Fairly quickly you will see what is important to the group as a whole. If there is an outlier sticky note with no other similar notes, then the issue is specific to that student and may not be a group norm. From these clusters, create anywhere from 5–7 norms the group can agree to (many more than seven can cause things to become confusing). It might look something like this:

- » Respect others' thoughts, actions, and ideas.
- » No teacher-bashing.
- » Everyone needs to contribute to the group.
- » Don't be mean.
- » Listen.
- » Don't be late.

Notice a few of these norms are negative in tone and include "no" and "don't." Try to encourage students to keep things in a positive tone. "No teacher bashing" becomes "Keep your criticism of teachers professional." "Don't be mean" becomes "Keep your comments positive," and "Don't be late" becomes "Be on time." Review the norms at the beginning of each advisory meeting. The group should police itself.

There may be times the advisory group wants to talk about things without a teacher in the room. This should be an option for the group. If appropriate, you should be willing to step out into the hallway until you are invited back in. This might allow students to open up even more and help each other with issues.

If you have a magnet program for gifted students, you can divide all of the students into advisory groups of no more than 20, providing a teacher to head up each one. You can even invite the principal and school counselor to lead a group to keep them small and intimate. Have advisory groups meet about every other week and be informal, where students bring up all of the issues, or there could be monthly themes that are discussed in the groups. A year full of topics might look something like this:

- » *September*: Getting into the swing of the school year.
- » *October*: Parents.
- » *November*: Homework/tests.
- » *December*: Nongifted peers.
- » *January*: Teachers.
- » *February*: Motivation/passion.
- » *March*: Career aspirations.
- » *April*: Perfectionism.
- » *May*: Transitions.

Or, you might use an existing structure, such as *The 7 Habits of Highly Effective Teens* by Sean Covey (2014). Each month a different habit could be focused on and talked about:

- » *Habit 1*: Be proactive.
- » *Habit 2*: Begin with the end in mind.
- » *Habit 3*: Put first things first.
- » *Habit 4*: Think win-win.

» *Habit 5*: Seek first to understand, then be understood.
» *Habit 6*: Synergize
» *Habit 7*: Sharpen the saw.

No matter how you decide to set up your advisory group, it is a nice outlet for students to have. Many times we focus only on the academic, so having some time carved out of the school day to allow them to address social-emotional needs will make for more balanced and well-adjusted students.

Strategy 3: Inquiry-Based Learning

To allow students who avoid taking risks to learn, a classroom needs to be a safe place. You need to create this environment—a place where it is okay to make mistakes. That means:
» allowing students the chance to rework material they did not master,
» not berating or teasing a student who gives the wrong answer in classroom discussion,
» not taking off points for an assignment being late,
» encouraging risk-taking,
» not grading homework,
» making sure there is a classroom management system in place where other students allow mistakes to be made, and
» making your own mistakes to show that this is okay.

If the only time you assess a student is when he is taking a high-stakes test, the student is going to feel that there is no wiggle room for mistakes because each one lowers his grade. There needs to be other opportunities to show the student has mastered the content other than just pencil-to-paper tests.

One way to encourage risk-taking in the classroom is to employ inquiry-based learning, which involves students pursuing topics they are interested in and exploring them more in depth. They must create a product that shows what they have learned about the topic. In a nutshell, it is learning by experiencing. Students are not just absorbing learning, but rather they are building it. In order to use inquiry learning in the classroom, there are a few conditions that have to be met (Grotzer, n.d.):

1. the environment must support risk-taking in learning,
2. the curriculum needs to allow for some uncertainty and ambiguity about exactly what children will learn, and
3. students need opportunities to learn forms of thinking that embody risk-taking and openness.

Consider a language arts class reading *The War of the Worlds* by H. G. Wells. There are tons of themes in the book, including foreignness, warfare, rules and order, community, exile, power, foolishness, fear, technology, modernization, fate, free will, etc. Have students pick a theme they are interested in learning more about. Different students will pick various themes that speak to them, meaning everyone in the class might be working on something different. You can even have them form groups based on their interests. Then, have students create essential questions for their chosen theme. For the theme of foreignness, for example:

1. How do people deal with foreignness when they first encounter the Martians?
2. The Martians are obviously foreign to the humans, but are there times in the book when the humans seem foreign to the Martians?
3. How does foreignness lead to war in the book?

Then, using these themes, have students create a radio broadcast that encapsulates them by drawing parallels to real-life incidents. A class discussion about Orson Welles's 1938 radio broadcast of *The War of the Worlds*, the use of propaganda, and the controversy it stirred up might be necessary. Students might add to their essential questions:

1. *How do people deal with foreignness when they first encounter the Martians?* Can you think of any instances in history where people have had similar experiences?
2. *The Martians are obviously foreign to the humans, but are there times in the book when the humans seem foreign to the Martians?* Do you see any parallels between this and our views on immigration and terrorism?

3. *How does foreignness lead to war in the book?* Can you draw a parallel to a historical war that was caused by foreignness?

During this process of inquiry-based learning, the classroom needs to be an environment that supports risk-taking. This means that (Grotzer, n.d.):

» question-asking is invited,
» "mistakes" are valued for the learning they provide and as natural parts of the inquiry process,
» open-ended questions are asked and appreciated,
» there's more than one possible answer,
» theorizing and considering evidence is considered more important than a "right answer,"
» sometimes questions are asked and not answered,
» all ideas are okay to share, and
» ideas are discussed for their explanatory potential, ability to solve the problem, and so on as opposed to being called "good" or "bad," "right" or "wrong" (Sec. II, para. 5).

Conclusion

Part of a teacher's job is to focus on the academics of his or her students, but equal attention should be paid to the social-emotional needs. If a seemingly bright student is becoming a behavior problem, reflect on the way the classroom is set up. Is the environment one in which the students can challenge the teacher in a productive manner, or one where the students feel safe to take risks? Having an outlet for students to share their feelings, such as an advisory group, can go a long way in making gifted students feel heard and understand they are not alone.

If you would like to read more in depth about one of these strategies or topics, a good resource is *I'm Not Just Gifted: Social-Emotional Curriculum for Guiding Gifted Children* by Christine Fonseca.

Cause 3

NOT HAVING PEERS

Students worry about social acceptance because everyone wants to belong. It is human nature—from the forming of tribes in prehistoric times to people who obsess over how many friends they have on Facebook. Compared to typical students, gifted children may have far fewer options for peers. A typical 8-year-old might want to talk about why dinosaurs are so cool, but a gifted 8-year-old might be curious about what caused their extinction or how they evolved. By definition of being gifted and being in the top 5% of their age-mates when it comes to cognitive ability, there are not a lot of kids like them. Depending on the district the student goes to, there might be even less than 5% of his or her age-mates to consider as peers.

This is why you often see gifted children, even younger ones, preferring the company of adults, such as their teacher. These are people they can have a conversation with. If they try to talk to age-mates who do not have similar interests, they become labeled as weird. James Delisle, in his book, *Parenting Gifted Kids: Tips for Raising Happy and Successful Children* (2006), talked about how many times gifted students do not feel normal. They are often labeled the opposite—but no child should be made to feel abnormal. A better term to use is *atypical*. Thus, gifted students who are trying to fit in sometimes make one of two decisions (Fonseca, 2016):

1. they hide their talents and try to fit in with the rest of the crowd, playing dumb to look cool; or
2. they take it to the other extreme and embrace their differences, becoming an outcast who is susceptible to bullying (p. 8).

Both of these situations need the careful eye of an educator who recognizes and offers the support needed. For the first, it takes a teacher who sees the potential in this student and helps coax it out without calling him out in front of his peers. If a teacher acknowledges publicly the intelligence of this student, he will just go deeper into his act, showing his friends he is just like them. Bullying, a nationwide epidemic for quite some time, requires a teacher who sees the atypical behavior of the gifted student as how she interacts with the world. The teacher should be teaching tolerance instead of trying to get the student to change in order to fit in. By trying to make them fit in, the teacher is devaluing the uniqueness of the child.

When Gifted Students Only Have Age-Mates

For many gifted children, there is a large difference between age-mates and those they would consider peer-mates. Age-mates are other children the same age as them. Growing up, students are often placed with their age-mates, whether it be for school, sports, or social reasons. This is done because they are usually the same age, with the same interests and hobbies. A gifted child, however, may not have the same interests and hobbies. Gifted students, with their advanced learning skills, might know everything there is to know about space, but an age-mate might not have the same body of knowledge. If you think about your own school career, how many times were you regularly mixed with children of different ages? Unless you went to a Montessori school where they mix grades into one large class, probably rarely. Schools, instead, advance students with their age-mates, making the assumption that these students have the most in common with those who were born around the same time. It would be more organic to allow children to stray into another grade in order to find common social and intellectual ground, but instead, students are shoehorned into the same grade and expected to find peers.

A peer is someone who shares the same passion, humor, and drive as you (Delisle, 2006). A peer-mate can many times be an age-mate, but there are times when this is not the case. This is especially the case with gifted children who find more in common with people older than them. The cruel trick society plays on these gifted students, however, is that older kids who might be their peer-mates do not want to hang around with a much younger kid. Essentially, these students are peerless. School can be a very lonely place for some children, and the lack of peers may cause a gifted child to begin to resent school. When this happens, he stops caring about school, which causes underachievement.

When Gifted Students Play Dumb to Fit In

Because they seek the approval of their peers, some gifted students hide their abilities. Why would they do this? Just listen to the announcements at any junior high or high school. They are rife with the accomplishments of sports, and yet rarely do they contain anything about academic accomplishments. The football stadium is full of people on Friday nights, but how many people attend an academic quiz bowl or come to watch the robotics team? How many media members are present when an athlete signs a letter of intent, and yet when a student receives an academic scholarship, no one reports that. We have trophy cases at the front of most schools, yet where are the acknowledgements for the academic endeavors, the very things schools are supposed to foster in children? Newspapers have a whole section reporting the daily results of high school athletics, yet how many articles are about the good academic work of students? You do not see Bill Gates or Stephen Hawking promoting soda in commercials. You see LeBron James and Kobe Bryant. It is way cooler to be a star athlete in your school than it is to be on the science Olympiad team. That being said, if an athletic science whiz has to choose between one or the other, which one do you think he is going to pick?

If a student wants to be socially accepted by his peers, he stands a much better chance of doing so through his athletic accomplishments than any academic ones. Most students can tell you the captain of the football team, but can they tell you who has the highest GPA in the class or who is taking the most AP courses? We show children time and time again that as a society we value athletics, as we worship professional athletes and pay them millions of dollars, so why wouldn't the social strata in schools reflect this worldview?

This is especially true with males, of whom more than 50% are underachievers (Weiss, 1972). This is because being smart does not fit the predominant macho image that prevails in junior high and high school. This desire to fit in by playing the role gifted students think will allow them to be accepted can cause them to suppress their academic abilities. It is simply not cool to be smart, so in order to meet these expectations, students play dumb, not reaching their potential.

When Gifted Students Are Bullied for Doing Well in Academics

Bullying is problem for kids of all ages. DoSomething.org (n.d.), a website devoted to the prevention of bullying, indicated that more than 3.2 million students in the United States are victims of bullying every year. Victims of this bullying come in all shapes and sizes, but it is especially prevalent toward gifted students. According to a study of 432 students in 11 states (Peterson & Ray, 2006), more than two thirds of academically talented eighth graders say they have been bullied at school. As a result, one in 10 children say they have tried to hide their science ability, and nearly one in five girls and more than one in 10 boys deliberately underachieve in math.

This bullying can be especially harsh on minority gifted students. Lisa M. Williams, coauthor of a study on bullying of high-achieving students, indicated the stereotype many hold about Black and Latino students is that they do not do well in school (as cited in American Sociological Association, 2011). Because they do not fall into this ste-reotype, high-achieving Black and Latino students may be especially vulnerable to bullies: Although all of the students who reported being bullied in the 10th grade saw a slight decrease in GPA by 12th grade, the change was more pronounced for Black and Latino students who tended to earn high grades (Huffington Post, 2011). Black students saw a 0.3-point GPA decrease in 12th grade from a 3.5 GPA in ninth grade, before they were bullied. High-achieving Latinos who were bullied experienced a 0.5-point drop in GPA from a 3.5 their freshman year (Cohn & Canter, 2003).

The effects of bullying are tough on any students, but, because of their increased intensity of emotions, gifted students may (Gordon, 2016):

1. view their academic gifts as flaws,
2. hide their giftedness,
3. take responsibility for the bullying,
4. become perfectionists,
5. experience strong reactions,
6. struggle to understand the bullying,
7. become self-critical, or
8. lose interest in school.

Many of these are causes of underachievement.

When Gifted Students Feel Bad for Being Smarter Than Peers

In the last chapter, the intensity of feelings of gifted children was discussed at length. Gifted students' feelings are magnified. So, if a gifted student gets angry, it might be more explosive than a nongifted child. On the other hand, if a gifted student has empathy for something, he or she has an intense feeling of empathy, which is why many gifted students worry about global problems. This also applies to empathy for their peers. When another child is having a bad day or is sad, a gifted child is likely to pick up on it and offer ways to help get the other student through it. The gifted child feels bad that one of his classmates is feeling bad. This empathy can sometimes expand to the point where a gifted student feels bad that he is smarter than a peer. In his mind, if he gets a question correct, it means that everyone else did not, and he might feel bad as a result. In order to let other students feel good about themselves, this gifted student will deliberately do poorly.

Practical Solutions

Strategy 1: Magnet Programs

Because gifted students have difficulty finding peer-mates amongst their age-mates, and the older students who could be their peer-mates do not want to associate with kids younger than them, the best chance of finding a peer-mate who is also an age-mate is by connecting with other gifted students. The problem is that the pool of gifted kids may be a small one. Because gifted students are in the top 5% of their age-mates when it comes to cognitive ability, 95% of other students are not a good match. Finding that student who also falls into the 5% can be a challenge.

Imagine a school district with seven elementary schools. At each of these schools is a handful of gifted students spread throughout the various classrooms in each building. At best you have two, maybe three, gifted students in a class together who can be viewed as peers. Sometimes there might just be one. What if you took all of these gifted students from all of the seven buildings and pull them into one program where they are together? This is called a magnet program, and it pulls all of the highly gifted students from the district, or maybe from the county, and puts them in one classroom. The teacher who is hired to teach these students would ideally be a gifted intervention specialist (GIS), and these students would be able to move at a much faster pace, because everyone in the class can process information at a quicker rate. In an even more perfect world, a district would have enough students to create a gifted team, with a different, highly qualified GIS teaching each subject.

There are many academic benefits to setting up a gifted magnet program, but the biggest advantage is putting a group of like-minded individuals together, providing them with peers. Students who usually feel atypical in other settings then feel typical. They see others who act like them, talk like them, and think like them. Things that were quirks to other children and teachers become commonplace, and the students feel accepted.

There are other benefits to having all of the gifted students together in a magnet program. You can:

» accelerate them as a group;

> » put them into advisory groups to address social-emotional needs;
> » focus professional development on teaching techniques especially effective at challenging gifted students, such as higher order thinking;
> » create competition, which can raise the bar;
> » go for depth rather than breadth of material;
> » identify a pool of potential National Merit Scholars;
> » mix them according to ability, not age;
> » expose them to academic extracurriculars, such as clubs;
> » provide academic rigor designed for higher level thinkers;
> » build a positive self-image;
> » nurture a small school community;
> » promote 21st-century survival skills;
> » develop leadership skills;
> » foster creativity; and
> » prepare them for high school, college, and beyond.

There are other models a magnet program can take depending on the available qualified teaching staff, resources, and cost.

Model 1. Students are pulled from various classes and grouped based on a single subject and offered a specialized curriculum designed to enhance their abilities and improve their skills. For example, there might be a math program for fifth graders where all of the gifted students from the school come to one class. It could be a language arts class or even a science class where they work on a specific program, such as robotics or Invention Convention/League. In order for this to be a gifted magnet program, it would be best if all of the students have been identified in the area of focus. You would most likely only need a single teacher to offer this class.

Model 2. Students are bussed to a single school, one day a week, in order to receive services with other gifted students. They attend their home school the other 4 days. This class could be enrichment where the teacher spends a majority of the time challenging students with projects and content that are not so subject-specific but rather crosscurricular. This would need a single teacher, a generalist. Because it is only one day a week, you might be able to offer it to many schools across the district depending on its size and demand.

Model 3. Eighth graders in the district all attend one school and have all academic subject areas offered to them. This grade is focused on because it is a transition year. In this case, students are getting ready to start high school, so the magnet program can be designed to meet the needs of these students, such as developing the study skills to handle rigorous high school courses like Advanced Placement (AP) or College Credit Plus (CCP). Students are shown the pathways available for students of their intellectual ability and counseled on what their paths might look like.

Model 4. The magnet school is comprised of several different grades. Students enter the program at its earliest grade and stay with the program until it runs its course. For example, a program could recruit students from grades 5–8. This magnet program is housed at one of the schools in the district and becomes a school within a school. The program can fall under the umbrella of the building principal, or a gifted coordinator can oversee its administrative responsibilities. In a program such as this, teachers would be subject-specific and loop with the students for multiple grades. The language arts teacher may teach fifth and sixth grade, but the social studies teacher might teach fifth through eighth. By looping, teachers really get to know the students and their capabilities, and are better able to challenge them in subsequent years.

Model 5. The district or county is large enough to make one of its schools a magnet gifted school. Students from around the district are transported to this school. Everyone, from the teachers to the administrators, to the support staff, such as counselors and psychologists, has been trained to work with gifted students. The curriculum, but also the unified arts, extracurricular activities, and the schedule are all designed with gifted students and their capabilities in mind. By setting up the magnet school in this manner, if you have a sixth grader doing eighth-grade math, she simply attends the eighth-grade math course at the time she would be in her sixth-grade class. Or you could have third and fourth graders in the same language arts class working at the same pace. This teaming model would allow the curriculum to be based on ability rather than age. And, because the entire school is designed like this, you do not have any awkwardness when a 10-year-old is in an eighth-grade math class with students 3 years older than him having conversations about things ahead of his development. Instead, there might be several students who qualify for the eighth-grade class as 10-year-olds, so there is a group of like-minded age-mates to relate to.

As beneficial as gifted magnet programs can be, there are realities associated with them. With so much money being spent toward special education, many states receive little to no funding for gifted programs, meaning a district would have to foot the bill. There are those who would argue that gifted magnet programs are elitist and are simply a method to further separate the haves from the have-nots. Would not all students, no matter their ability, benefit from a program such as this? Magnet programs, however, are especially valuable to gifted students because they provide a community of gifted learners where these students are able to locate peer-mates as well as age-mates.

Strategy 2: Cluster Grouping

A more cost-effective way of placing gifted students with others like them is cluster grouping. Four to six gifted students are assigned to a heterogeneous classroom within their grade. This within-class grouping places gifted students with students of other achievement levels but not too wide a range. The teacher then differentiates within her classroom, allowing her to meet the needs of these gifted students and for gifted students to have peer-mates.

Table 4 is an example of several classrooms where cluster grouping is possible. Cluster grouping cuts down on the amount of differentiation a teacher has to do. In this scenario, the teacher of each class only has to differentiate for three skill levels. In Class 1, the teacher just has to worry about gifted, average, and below average. The five gifted students grouped into this class will have a good chance of finding someone who thinks like they do. Notice how there are no far-below-average students in this class. The teacher can challenge the gifted students without having to worry about remediation. He could address this with station rotations designed to challenge students at the different levels or projects that are scaffolded across the three levels. Similarly, the teacher

TABLE 4

Sample Classrooms Where Cluster Grouping Is Possible

30 Students Per Class	Gifted	High Achievers	Average	Below Average	Far Below Average
Class 1	5	0	15	10	0
Class 2	0	5	15	10	0
Class 3	0	5	15	0	10

in Class 3 only has to concern herself with high-achieving, average, and far-below-average students. Then, her strategies would differentiate across these skill levels. You will notice in this scenario there are no high achievers placed in the classroom with the gifted students.

Without cluster grouping, the gap in the classroom between abilities becomes much wider, making it more difficult because the middle moves. Figure 7 is an example of a classroom with a lot of varying abilities. Notice the special education and gifted students begin to get pulled thin while the majority of learning is going in the middle. If you group students with higher abilities in a class together, the spectrum looks Figure 8. Because the gap is not as wide, the gifted are closer to the crux of learning.

It is important to have the right teacher with the right cluster of students. Look back at Table 4. In Class 1, you would want someone who is a trained gifted intervention specialist. However, depending on the state, these can be hard to come by. If you cannot have a GIS in the position, having a teacher with a track record of working successfully with high-level thinking students would be best. In order for a clustering group to be successful (Rogers, 1991):

» the teacher must receive specialized training,
» the teacher must be motivated to work with gifted children,
» the curriculum for the cluster must be appropriately differentiated, and
» the remainder of the class cannot contain difficult or demanding students.

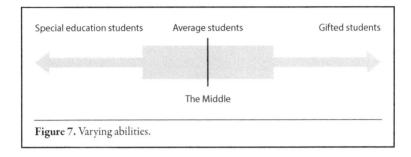

Figure 7. Varying abilities.

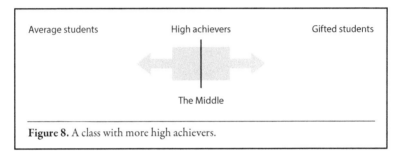

Figure 8. A class with more high achievers.

The first three all have to do with having the right teacher in the gifted cluster. The last key for success deals with the grouping of the students.

Table 5 shows what it looks like when students are spread across the classrooms more evenly. In this alignment, the teacher has to be able to differentiate over five different skill levels. This makes it much more difficult, and many times, because it is such a wide expanse, teachers teach to the middle. In this case, the teacher will be focused on the average student with the far-below-average students having to catch up, but the couple of gifted students will be bored because they are not being challenged.

The main benefit of clustering is its economic advantage. Other advantages include (Winebrenner & Brulles, 2008):
  » challenging gifted students every day, all day;
  » creating learning and leadership opportunity for *all* students;
  » empowering all teachers by expanding awareness and providing preparation;
  » ongoing assessment of students' strengths and needs; and
  » providing all students with opportunities for extended learning.

TABLE 5

Sample Classrooms Where Cluster Grouping Is More Difficult

30 Students Per Class	Gifted	High Achievers	Average	Below Average	Far Below Average
Class 1	2	4	15	7	3
Class 2	2	3	15	7	3
Class 3	1	3	15	6	4

In addition to challenging gifted students, a cluster will give them more opportunities to find like-minded peers with whom they can relate.

Strategy 3: Acceleration

Although acceleration is not as effective as having a gifted magnet school, it is more cost-effective. Acceleration is sort of like an a la carte version of gifted services for gifted students who are able to move through content at a quicker pace than others. This can come in a variety of forms:

» grade skipping;
» early entrance to kindergarten;
» college-level classes such as AP, CCP, or International Baccalaureate (IB); and
» subject-based acceleration.

Accelerated students are usually placed in classes with older students who are handling more advanced curriculum. Because they are in these classes with peers rather than age-mates, these students can find people who are academically on the same level, giving them something in common to talk about. A student who is particularly skilled in math might be able to breeze through his ninth-grade algebra curriculum. He is then is placed in a 10th-grade geometry class so that the level of the curriculum lines up with his ability. This becomes easier at the high school level with so many choices for classes and different pathways for students to take. It is more challenging for younger students where classes are more prescribed. If a fourth-grade student is ready for fifth-grade math, but in his or her district, fifth grade is at the middle school, is the district going to bus the student from the elementary school over to the middle school for that one class? Most likely not. That is why a gifted magnet program can be the ideal choice.

There is a misconception that having a child skip a grade or content can be harmful to her social-emotional needs. Countless studies have shown, however, that more often than not, skipping is going to result in a good experience for the child: In a study of high-ability children who had been accelerated, 71% reported satisfaction with their acceleration experience (Lubinski, Webb, Morelock, & Benbow, 2001). Of the participants who reported they were unsatisfied, the majority indicated they would have preferred more acceleration.

These students are able to find like-minded peers and actually begin to develop a higher self-concept, both academically and socially. Lee, Olszewski-Kubilius, and Thomson (2012) studied a sample of students who had been whole-grade accelerated. They found that the students who were younger in age than their peers were not different in their perceived interpersonal competence. They were able to make friends just as easily as the typical students, perhaps more easily than if they had not been accelerated, because they were now with peer-mates.

Conclusion

The strategies shared in this chapter would be challenging for a teacher to implement alone. More than likely, you will want your building administrator, gifted services coordinator, or curriculum department to help figure out which model works best for your district. The benefits of putting gifted students with others like them have been studied at length. A study by Steenbergen-Hu, Makel, and Olszewski-Kubilius (2016) found that:

> » In comparison to their peers who received traditional non-ability-grouped instruction, students benefited from within-class grouping, which often involves teachers assigning students to several small homogeneous groups for instruction based on prior achievement or learning capacities.

>> The benefits were even greater when students were grouped across grade levels for specific subjects, especially reading, and when high-achieving and gifted students were grouped together for instruction.

>> Students who accelerated their learning through various methods, such as skipping grades, taking Advanced Placement (AP) courses and exams, or entering school or college earlier, significantly outperformed their non-accelerated peers of the same age, and performed just as well as older students who were not accelerated. (para. 4)

Ultimately, having children in a gifted magnet program gives students the best chance to find age-mates who are also peer-mates. Cluster grouping will give children a few students they might be able to relate to, while acceleration will find them peer-mates but not necessarily age-mates. A gifted magnet program, especially one that services multiple grades, will create a larger pool of peers.

If you would like to read more in depth about one of these strategies or topics, a good resource is *Total School Cluster Grouping and Differentiation: A Comprehensive, Research-Based Plan for Raising Student Achievement and Improving Teacher Practices* by Marcia Gentry.

Cause 4

HOME LIFE

How important is the influence of home life on a child's education? Academic research finds no correlation with the amount of money spent on a child's education and educational gains. In other words, spending more money toward a child's education does not necessarily make him or her do better. But there is a correlation between parental influences and educational outcomes. If parents are involved in their child's education and show they care, school readiness and even likelihood of college completion increase (Hanushek, 1997). Over the past 4 decades, taking inflation out of the equation, public spending of money on education has increased by 128% (Lips, 2008). However, the achievement of these students has remained stagnant. Families, on the other hand, have seen a decline in the number of children growing up in households with their biological parents. In 1960, 88% of children lived with two parents, but, by 2016, that number dropped to 69% (Amato, 2005). It is estimated that one child in two will spend some part of his or her childhood in a single-parent home (Bumpass & Sweet, 1989).

Here are some more statistics about the effects of home life on students' education (Kim, 2008):

» First-graders whose mothers were married when they were born are less likely to engage in disruptive behavior with peers and teachers than those whose mothers were single or cohabiting at the time of their birth.

» Children aged 3 to 12 who live in intact families have higher average math scores than peers whose mothers live in cohabiting relationships.

» Children aged 7 to 10 who live in continuously intact families tend to score higher on reading tests than peers who have lived in other family structures.
» Children aged 6 to 11 who live in intact families tend to be more engaged in their schoolwork than peers in other family structures.
» Middle school and high school students who experience a parental divorce tend to suffer declines in their grade point averages and are more likely to fail a course one year later compared to peers of married parents. (pp. 4–5)

Given the importance of home life on the education of a child, there are several things that can inhibit a child from doing his best in school and thus lead to underachievement.

When Parents May Not Value Education

As much as teachers would like to believe that every parent wants the best education possible for his or her child, the harsh reality is that this is not always the case. There are a variety of reasons that a parent does not value his or her child getting an education. Sometimes it comes from the fact that, as children, the parents did not receive a quality education. They see school as a place of bad memories, where they might have been bullied, disciplined, disrespected, or ridiculed. They come to view school as a bad place, and this reflects in the way their child sees school as well.

Then, there are those parents who wish to provide their child with a quality education but do not have the resources to tap into this value. They either lack the social capital, money, or access to good schools that would provide a quality education. It is our nation's worst-kept secret that the performance of students on achievement tests and the socioeconomic status of a school community usually go hand in hand. Students who come from an affluent school system more often than not score better than students from an urban or rural school with a lower socioeconomic status.

There are other parents who do not know how to get involved in their child's education. This can happen in households where English is a second language. Because the parents do not speak fluent English, they often feel inadequate when it comes to school due to the language barrier, cultural differences, or their own lack of education. This creates the perception that these parents do not care because they do not come to school events or attend parent-teacher conferences. The reality might be that they are not made to feel culturally welcome, so they avoid such events. Traditional methods of communicating with parents—mail, phone, or e-mail—might not be the best way to communicate with them. Also, the traditional times we plan for school events and parent-teacher conferences, in the evenings or right after school, might not work with parents' schedules. Schools need to consider that, when it appears a parent does not care, the problem may be that the environment the school has created is not conducive for these parents to be involved. Alternatives need to be considered, such as conducting home visits, arranging for parent-teacher conferences at a more convenient place for parents, such as a meeting room at an apartment complex where many of the students live, or holding meetings in the morning or the middle of the day.

You cannot make parents value education, but you can help them see the value for their child and the opportunities an education will provide for them.

When Parents' Expectations Are Too High

As much as teachers want parents to be involved in their child's education, there is such a thing as being too involved. Involvement is definitely good. Students whose parents are more willing to help them with school are more likely to have higher levels of academic achievement and psychosocial development with lower levels of deviant behavior and psychological problems than peers whose parents are not as highly responsive (Fletcher, Steinberg, & Sellers, 1999). Parents who are too involved, however, can cause problems. These helicopter parents are so involved that they do not provide their children the space needed to learn. In *The Overachievers: The Secret Lives of Driven Kids* (Robbins, 2006), one of the profiled students is nicknamed "AP Frank." As a junior and senior he is enrolled in all AP classes at the insistence of his mother, who has really high expectations for him, even managing his time to the point of abuse. His parent is so involved that he cannot wait to go to college the next year just so he can get away from her iron fist and have a social life.

If a parent pushes a student too hard, the student might rebel in the only way that might seem available to him: doing poorly in school. Parents should certainly have high expectations for their gifted child. Otherwise, some students might just stay in their comfort zone and not learn much. There is, however, a balance between setting high standards and putting undue pressure on a child. How does a parent maintain this balance? According to psychologist Peggy Tsatsoulis (2002–2017), you can share the following tips with parents:

1. *Self-reflect*: Ask yourself why it is important for you to push your child. Make sure the answer is the honest one, not the one that makes you look the best. Determine where your child is academically and where you want him or her to be. Seek advice on what this looks like from teachers and family friends. Sometimes your expectation might be unrealistic. We all want our children to be the best, but sometimes they are capable of only so much.

2. *Practice acceptance*: Know your child and what he or she is capable of, and adjust your expectations. For example, B's may be acceptable in math because you know your student often struggles with the concepts and formulas.

3. *Have regular conversations with your child*: These do not need to be a formal family meeting. Talk to your child in the car on the way to picking up a pizza or while going for a walk together. Ask him or her what he or she needs from you and if he or she feels you put too much pressure on him or her. He or she will likely give you honest feedback.

4. *Pay attention*: Look at what is going on right in front of you. Actions can speak louder than words. If your child is saying everything is all right, but you notice changes in his or her

behavior, this might be reason to take notice. Pay attention to eating and sleeping habits, the kinds of friends he or she hangs out with, as well as the consistency in his or her grades.

5. *Speak with your child's teachers and/or counselor*: Your child's teachers are the best source for getting information. Besides yourself, they are the adult your child is spending the most time with. When you do communicate, ask the teacher how you can be supportive to the academic process. Ask the teacher how much help he expects for you to give your child on homework. Counselors are another resource available to you. They have tools and tips to help you be a support system to your child.

6. *Relax and know*: Everything will work out (para. 4–9).

When Home Dynamics Are a Problem

There are various home dynamics that can lead to underachievement (see Table 6). There are things a teacher can control concerning the education of his students, and things that are completely out of his hands. He can control the discipline in his classroom, the expectations he sets for his students, and the dedication and passion he shows toward teaching his students. What he cannot control is the home life of the students. Rather than trying to control something not in your control, you need to focus on what you can. Most of the factors in Table 6 are out of your control, but you can be the one thing most of the students are seeking—someone who cares about them.

Practical Solutions

Strategy 1: Before- or Afterschool Enrichment Clubs

Provide opportunities for students to participate in clubs designed to enrich their learning. If students are coming from a home life where they feel as though they do not belong, these clubs provide a place where

TABLE 6

Home Dynamics That Lead to Underachievement

Tends to Cause *Episodic* Underachievement	Tends to Cause *Chronic* Underachievement
Dysfunction	Economic status
Father-son relationship	Attitude toward school and jobs
Family disruption	Language
Parent discord	Ethnic differences
	Motivation modeling

Note. Adapted from Shelagh Gallagher, personal communication, August 2017. Adapted with permission of the author.

they do. These clubs can be held before or after school, depending on what works best with the advisor's schedule. Some districts actually pay stipends for people who run clubs.

Clubs can come in a variety of forms, such as one that is an extension of the advisor's passion, something that the advisor is involved in and wants to pass on to students. For example, you might be really into anime, so you start an anime club that meets to view anime movies, read manga, draw or create anime, or play tabletop games, such as shogi, go, and mahjong. Or, if you are really into the environment, you could start an eco club that focuses on ways to help the school and/or the community to be more environmentally sound.

Another option would be to create clubs that may not be your passion, but are something you could competently run and are proven to enrich gifted students, such as chess, creative writing, mock trial, robotics, art, debate, investment, drama, coding, gaming, gardening, etc. These clubs could be as structured or unstructured as you want. For example, chess club could just be a place for students to come together and play chess. All an advisor would have to provide are the boards and pieces. A more involved chess club might teach strategy, learn new techniques, and attend tournaments. The real goal of the club is to provide a place students can go and feel as though they are cared for. Students would also learn a new skill and develop leadership and collaboration skills.

Rather than reinventing the wheel, a third option is using a national program, as they tend to have a rich curriculum of activities and culminating events to do with students. Some of these programs include Model United Nations, Invention Convention/League, Battle of the Books, and MATHCOUNTS. These programs have students from all over the country participating with state and regional competitions.

For example, Destination Imagination (DI) is a global program for grades K–12 that has students pick a challenge. They register nationally and receive a passport number and materials for that challenge. The students must then create a skit that demonstrates the elements of the challenge as well as specific skills. There are various challenges to choose from—technical, scientific, engineering, fine arts, improvisation, outreach—each with a different theme. All challenges require students to be creative in the manner in which they solve their challenge as well as prepare and perform their skit. After preparing for several months, teams register with a local affiliate and take part in a regional tournament that pulls teams from the area. The teams that score the best on their challenge then are invited to go to the state competition. From there the best teams go to the global competition held in Knoxville, TN. It does involve some coordination on the part of the teacher or team manager, but the parameters of the challenge, the tournament, the judging, and the awards are all handled by the organization.

Table 7 is a list of some of the major national competitions that teachers can create a club around. Because these organizations have been doing these competitions for years, it would be a matter of connecting with the state or local affiliate, figuring out what exactly is involved with participating, and providing the resources for students to be able to prepare for the competition.

Strategy 2: Parent Education Sessions

Parents don't know what they don't know—especially when it comes to gifted students. Giving them just a little bit of education about working with their gifted child can go a long way. Having a series of parent workshops would allow you to introduce issues prevalent amongst gifted students in a safe place, where instead of being accusatory, it allows

TABLE 7

National Competitions for Student Clubs and Enrichment

Competition	Age Range/Grades	Area of Study
American Mathematics Competitions (http://www.maa.o-g/math-competitions)	Grades 8–12	Math
America's Battle of the Books (http://www.battleoftheboo=s.org)	Grades 3–12	English language arts
Egg Drop Contest	Grades 5–12	Science, engineering
FIRST LEGO League (http://www.firstlegoleague.org)	Ages 9–16	Science, engineering
Future City Competition (http://futurecity.org)	Grades 6–8	Science, technology, engineering, math
Future Problem Solving Program International (http://www.fpspi.org)	Ages 8–18	Logic, global connections
Invention League's Convention Program (http://www.inventionleague.org)	Grades K–8	Science, engineering
Linguistics Olympiad (http://www.nacloweb.org)	Grades 6–12	English language arts
MATHCOUNTS (https://www.mathcounts.org)	Grades 6–8	Math, reasoning
Math League (http://www.mathleague.com)	Grades 3–6	Math

TABLE 7, *Continued.*

Competition	Age Range/Grades	Area of Study
Math Olympiads (http://www.moems.org)	Grades 4–8	Math
Model United Nations (http://www.unausa.org/global-classrooms-model-un)	High school, some states have junior high	Social studies, global awareness
Odyssey of the Mind (https://www.odysseyofthemind.com)	Grades K–12	Problem solving, creativity
PhysicsBowl (https://www.aapt.org/Programs/PhysicsBowl)	High school	Science
Power of the Pen (http://www.powerofthepen.org)	Grades 7–8	English language arts
NASA Ames Space Settlement Contest (https://settlement.arc.nasa.gov/Contest)	Grades 7–12	Science, technology, engineering, math
National Shakespeare Competition (https://www.esuus.org/esu/programs/shakespeare_competition)	Grades 9–12	English language arts, performing arts
Science Olympiad (https://www.soinc.org)	Grades 6–12	Science
Siemens Competition in Math, Science, & Technology (https://siemenscompetition.discoveryeducation.com)	Grades 9–12	Science, technology, engineering, math
WordMasters Challenge (http://www.wordmasterschallenge.com)	Grades 3–8	English language arts, reasoning

85

parents to arrive at a realization themselves. Hopefully, at this presentation, a discussion will occur where parents are talking about their children and some of the struggles and successes they have encountered. This in itself can be an education, and it is always easier to hear from other parents rather than from a perceived authority figure.

Your parent education sessions could take many forms. Topics you might want to address include:

- » myths about giftedness,
- » underachievement,
- » social-emotional needs,
- » creativity,
- » outside learning opportunities,
- » summer enrichment,
- » challenging reads,
- » the gifted brain,
- » emotional intelligence,
- » developing self-concept,
- » identification and assessment of gifted, and
- » college and career readiness.

Although you cannot control a student's home life, you can seek to teach the parents what a supportive home life would look like. Suggestions you could provide to parents in education sessions include (Siegle, 2006):

- » Modeling their own curiosity about the world around them. Parents must demonstrate how curiosity is transformed into action. For example, a question about the number of moons orbiting Saturn might lead to looking up the answer on the Internet or in an encyclopedia.
- » Nurturing their children's curiosity and love of learning through opportunities outside of school that help them explore their interests.
- » Letting their children know that they value school and showing them how their school experiences are important now and will prove useful in the future.

» Monitoring their children's homework, which sends the message that parents value what their children do in school.

» Sharing their children's interests with the school and working with the school and their children to tie these interests to school projects.

» Talking about their children's giftedness with them by helping them recognize that they are continually changing and growing and that they have a hand in their own accomplishments and growth.

» Documenting their children's growth by saving their schoolwork or videotaping them performing various tasks and sharing these items with them later. The children will be impressed with how much progress they have made.

» Helping them understand that challenging situations are opportunities to acquire or improve skills and that encountering difficulty does not mean that they are not intelligent.

» Helping children recognize the part that effort has played in their growth by complimenting them with specific examples. A general compliment, such as "Good work," is not as effective as, "Your studying paid off—now you really know the periodic table."

» Creating opportunities for their children to interact with role models. Students' expectations are based on the experiences of their parents and role models.

» Discussing cause-and-effect relationships with their children. In particular, parents can counsel children faced with difficult situations on how to change the environment to fit their needs, how to achieve success by adjusting to the existing environment, or when to let go of a fruitless idea or hopeless situation (para. 2–6).

Another parent-education opportunity is a book study. An excellent resource for this is James Delisle's *Parenting Gifted Kids: Tips for Raising Happy and Successful Children* (2006). You could have parents read chapters over the course of a school year, hosting a meeting every few chapters or so, getting together as a group and talking about it. For those parents who are unable to attend, the discussion could either be filmed and put online, or notes could be sent out.

Gifted parents certainly do not want to be preached at or told they are doing something wrong. These parents of gifted children, many who are gifted themselves, like to learn, so teaching some strategies they could use at home would be an effective way to improve students' home life.

Strategy 3: Field Trips

Many students who come from supportive homes do a lot of enrichment as a family. They take trips to the zoo and talk about the various ecosystems, go to the art museum and compare paintings, or attend the science center to learn fun ways to use electricity. Statistics show that children from higher socioeconomic homes tend to participate in these sorts of enrichment activities more often than children from lower socioeconomic households. Malcolm Gladwell, in his book *Outliers* (2008), discussed a study conducted by Karl Alexander at Johns Hopkins University, which discovered what was termed a summer learning gap. Two students from polar opposite socioeconomic households achieved at about the same rate within the school year. Upon returning to school the following year, however, the student from the higher socioeconomic household gained learning over the summer because of the experiences his or her parents provided. Schools could close this gap a little, but each summer it happened again and again, causing the gap to become so large that by the ninth grade there was no closing it. There was a correlation between those students who received these out-of-school learning experiences and those who took college preparatory classes and even those who went on to a 4-year college.

In order to level the playing field a little, arrange to take students on field trips. There are three ways to approach them.

Approach 1: During-school field trip tied to curriculum. A history teacher is beginning a unit on slavery. In order to deepen the level of understanding of the students, he makes arrangements for his students to attend the National Underground Railroad Museum in Cincinnati, OH, where there are multiple exhibits, films, reenactments, and even an actual cabin that used to house slaves. This experience is beyond anything students could get by reading textbooks for weeks, and it is all in a single day. Not only that, it provides an experience for some students whose parents would not have the resources or time to take them to such a museum. Students are then accountable for what they learn on the field trip because it is part of the curriculum, which is demonstrated in either a project, a reflection, or an assessment.

Approach 2: Weekend or summer field trips. A field trip need not be tied to the school day in order to be meaningful and provide enrichment. Going to an arboretum and experiencing the various types of trees and plants can be enriching even if it is not linked to the curriculum. Or, taking students to an observatory where they can see the stars and planets, as well as learn how scientists study them, might be life altering, as a student leaves there wanting to be an astronomer. Keep in mind, field trips are an experience, and for many students, they are an experience they would normally not have. Being able to offer these sort of field trips on the weekend or during the summer, the time when other children might be experiencing these on their own and jumping ahead of their peers, puts students on equal footing.

Approach 3: Bring the field trip to the students. Field trips can be expensive for a school district. Not only is there the cost to attend, but there is also a cost for busing and finding chaperones, and the emergency medical forms, not to mention the moving of several kids from place to place, can sometimes feel like herding cats. What if you could have all of the benefits of a field trip without actually having to physically go anywhere? There are a couple of alternatives. One of these is that many people and organizations, such as the zoo, science center, performing arts groups, or visiting authors, have outreach programs where they actually come to schools. Rather than trying to transport hundreds of children many miles away, the venue or speaker will come to the school.

Another option is to take virtual field trips. There is amazing technology where students can explore the ancient Pyramid of Giza, go swimming with sharks, or tour the Louvre in Paris. Students use virtual reality goggles that look just like the View-Masters of our childhoods. A classroom set can be purchased for the district and circulated to various teachers. Although they may not be as good as actually going to a destination, these sorts of field trips allow you to cover more distance and see things that even well-to-do families might not be able to experience.

The final option is to have students create a field trip for others. This would involve students creating museum exhibits covering various topics, as seen in Figure 9. The class can go online and study real museum exhibits to see how they look. Once students set up their exhibits, you can invite other classes to come visit the museum, providing a field trip for those in your school.

Conclusion

There is very little you can do to control a student's home life. But most students from nonsupportive households are looking for someone who cares. That is something you can control. Caring about their academic achievements in the classroom and offering opportunities to belong by supervising a club or providing a field trip, can go a long way in making an impact on the lives of these underachieving students.

If you would like to read more in-depth about one of these strategies or topics, a good resource is *Parenting Gifted Kids: Tips for Raising Happy and Successful Children* by James Delisle.

Purpose

You are charged with creating an exhibit in the Egyptian Museum.

You are responsible for a certain aspect of Egyptian culture. You must create a display so that someone coming to the museum could learn everything they could about the aspect of culture. This means you will need an artifact(s) of some sort, whether it be a model, poster, trifold, video reenactment, etc. There need to be labels as well as an exhibit title. Like any good museum, you will need to have a sign that explains the exhibit in detail based on the research you find.

Summary

The theme of this museum is how the river shaped this aspect of culture, so somewhere in the exhibit this will need to be explained.

Recommendation

Your exhibit will be evaluated on three aspects:
- Artifact/Display
- Content of Research
- Professionalism

Figure 9. Sample museum exhibit assignment.

Cause 5

TWICE-
EXCEPTIONALITY

Oftentimes, gifted students and students with disabilities are seen as two opposite ends of a spectrum. There are children who fall into both categories, however. These children are referred to as twice-exceptional.

It is double the challenge to educate twice-exceptional students. They must receive instruction that attends to both their gifts and their disabilities. This is no easy task, because many times it is the learning disability that receives the focus. On top of that, because of their giftedness, these children are prime candidates for underachievement because their learning disabilities make it difficult for them to reach their high potential.

There are typically three categories of twice-exceptional students (Besnoy, 2006):

1. *Identified gifted*: These are children who have slight learning disabilities, allowing them to be recognized as gifted by educators. This is because they are able to test well on the achievement and cognitive tests. Their giftedness, however, masks their learning disabilities, so they struggle in school. Teachers may encourage them to work harder, but what these students really need are interventions tailored to their learning disability.

2. *Identified learning disabled*: These children are the opposite; they have a learning disability, and this prevents them from being identified as gifted. The services these children receive are simply for their disability, so their giftedness is never addressed. The focus is on their disabilities and not their giftedness, so

these students oftentimes do not receive the challenge their gifted minds require.

3. *Unidentified gifted and learning disabled:* These are the children whose giftedness and learning disability mask one another. In other words, the learning disability prevents them from being identified as gifted, and being gifted prevents them from being identified as learning disabled. Because of this, they are almost never identified as either. They go through school maintaining good, not great, grades, making recognition of both their giftedness and their disabilities very difficult.

When teachers are writing Individualized Education Plans (IEPs) for a special education student, they usually focus on the student's weaknesses and what can be provided that will allow him to achieve despite them. With gifted students, teachers and coordinators often identify based on a student's strengths. He is gifted in math or he is superior cognitive, so he can think at a much higher level and thus should be challenged.

Working with twice-exceptional students, focus on their strengths. Oftentimes their strengths can compensate for their weaknesses. This is a precarious balancing act that, if done properly, can result in the student achieving to his potential. If it is unbalanced or not properly carried out, underachievement can result.

When Learning Disabilities Affect Learning

There are several types of learning disabilities that can affect the way a student is able to process material or learn. Some of the more common ones are (Besnoy, 2006):

» *Dyslexia:* This condition affects a child's ability to read. It causes students to struggle with memorization of facts, reading comprehension, and organizing language both written and spoken.

» *Dyscalculia:* This causes students to have difficulty mentally organizing mathematical operational procedures. They might have trouble recognizing mathematical symbols and can reverse numbers. This learning disability causes one to have only modest knowledge of his or her cognitive strategies.

» *Dysgraphia*: These students have difficulty with word recognition, fine motor skills, and orthographic-motor integration. This seriously hinders a child's ability to write. They can also find it difficult to process language and spell.

» *Speech/language disorders*: These can cause students to lack appropriate listening comprehension skills, which basically means they struggle with following verbal directions. This can cause gaps in knowledge and difficulty with social situations.

Although the disability might vary, the characteristics of gifted students with learning disabilities commonly include (Reis, Neu, & McGuire, 1995):

» frustration with inability to master certain academic skills,
» learned helplessness,
» general lack of motivation,
» disruptive classroom behavior,
» perfectionism,
» supersensitivity,
» failure to complete assignments,
» lack of organizational skills,
» demonstration of poor listening and concentration skills,
» deficiency in tasks emphasizing memory and perceptual abilities,
» low self-esteem,
» unrealistic self-expectations, and
» absence of social skills with some peers (p. 17).

Many of these characteristics mirror what underachievers without a learning disability have, such as perfectionism, lack of organizational skills, and supersensitivity. There are others specific to twice-exceptional students, such as deficiency in tasks emphasizing memory and perceptual abilities, demonstration of poor listening and concentration skills, and frustration with inability to master certain academic skills.

As stated before, it is important not to focus on the disabilities that hamper the learning, but rather the strengths these students bring to the classroom. Some of these strengths include (Reis et al., 1995):

>> advanced vocabulary use,
>> exceptional analytic abilities,
>> high levels of creativity,
>> advanced problem-solving skills,
>> ability to think of divergent ideas and solutions,
>> specific aptitude (artistic, musical, or mechanical),
>> wide variety of interests,
>> good memory,
>> task commitment, and
>> spatial abilities (p. 18).

The teacher working with this student should try to identify the student's strengths. This can be done by simply asking the student himself what he believes are his strengths:

>> What do you do well?
>> What do you struggle with?
>> If you could improve any academic skill, what would it be and why?
>> If you could improve any social skill, what would it be and why?
>> What excites you about school?
>> What do you find boring at school?
>> If you could change anything at school, what would it be?
>> What are some effective ways teachers have taught you in the past?
>> What doesn't work for you?
>> What do you most like to learn about?
>> What is something you would like to learn more about?

It is important to get a good understanding of the student's strengths before deciding which strategies to use with him.

When Twice-Exceptional Students Have Attention Deficit/Hyperactivity Disorder

In addition to a learning disability, a neurologically-based developmental disability can also make a child twice-exceptional. About 3%–5% of children have Attention Deficit/Hyperactivity Disorder (ADHD), and it causes a child's attention process to become disrupted and to be easily distractible. This might manifest itself in various ways, through inattention, hyperactivity, impulsivity, or a combination (American Psychiatric Association, 2013).

Inattention is when a child has great difficulty concentrating on a task (especially if it is boring or long term). Some students might struggle to figure out just where to start a task. Because they cannot figure it out, they are never able to move forward. Others might be able to start, but once in, they get lost along the way, especially if there are a lot of steps. Some behaviors that might indicate inattention include (American Psychiatric Association, 2013):

>» failing to give close attention to details or making careless mistakes in schoolwork, work, or other activities;
>» having difficulty sustaining attention in tasks or play activities;
>» not seeming to listen when spoken to directly;
>» not following through on instructions and failing to finish schoolwork, chores, or duties in the workplace (not due to oppositional behavior or failure to understand instructions);
>» having difficulty organizing tasks and activities;
>» avoiding, disliking, or being reluctant to engage in tasks that require sustained mental effort (such as schoolwork or homework);
>» losing things necessary for tasks or activities (e.g., toys, school assignments, pencils, books, or tools);
>» getting easily distracted by extraneous stimuli; and
>» being forgetful in daily activities.

Hyperactivity is when a student appears to be in constant motion, may be fidgety and restless, or gets easily excited. Because the student does not know how to cope with this hyperactivity, she may have difficulty keeping her focus and getting her schoolwork done. For the teacher, this hyperactivity is a behavior issue, but as with most handicaps, the student is not in total control. This behavior is not a choice; it is a disorder that impedes her learning. Some signs of hyperactivity include (American Psychiatric Association, 2013):

> » constant fidgeting with hands or feet or squirming in seat;
> » leaving seat in classroom or in other situations in which remaining seated is expected;
> » running about or climbing excessively in situations in which it is inappropriate;
> » having difficulty playing or engaging in leisure activities quietly;
> » often being "on the go" or acting as if "driven by a motor"; and
> » talking excessively.

The final symptom of ADHD is impulsivity. As discussed earlier, some gifted children are impulsive. The answer comes so quickly to them in their fast-thinking minds, that it is out of their mouths in seconds. The impulsivity in children with ADHD is different. Impulsive gifted children act without thinking because they struggle to wait or delay gratification. The impulsive behavior of children with ADHD verges on risk-taking, which in certain circumstances can be dangerous. It may cause a child to dive into the deep end of the pool or, when dared by a classmate, jump off the monkey bars. In reality, this child is not a risk-taker, but simply cannot control the impulsivity. This child often may (American Psychiatric Association 2013):

> » blurt out answers before questions have been completed,
> » have difficulty awaiting a turn, and
> » interrupt or intrude on others (e.g., butt into conversations or games).

An educator should understand that these behaviors are not a matter of choice. These children have little control over these behaviors, although there are medications that can help students to manage them.

When Twice-Exceptional Students Have Autism Spectrum Disorders

Autism spectrum disorders (ASD) are complex disorders of the brain that vary in severity but are usually characterized by difficulties in social interaction, repetitive behaviors, and trouble with verbal and nonverbal communication. The intensity of ASD can be greater for some kids than others. Children with severe ASD rarely test as gifted because the disorder masks the giftedness. However, many students who have high-functioning autism do qualify as gifted. This is because gifted students and children with high-functioning autism have many of the same behaviors. Some of these include (Neihart, 2000):

» verbal fluency,
» excellent memories,
» fascination with letters or numbers,
» demonstrating an absorbing interest in a specialized topic,
» annoying peers by talking so much about their interests,
» asking endless questions,
» giving lengthy responses, and
» hypersensitivity to sensory stimuli.

Differences that might separate gifted students from twice-exceptional students with ASD include speech patterns, response to routines, humor, and motor clumsiness (Neihart, 2000). It is these differences that the teacher must learn to work with in order to get the most out of the high-functioning autistic child's gifts.

Practical Solutions

Strategy 1: Teach Organization Skills

Gifted children typically are not the most organized. You may ask them to get a homework assignment for you, and they pull out a binder jam-packed with various papers, some of which date back to the Reagan administration. Their desks are always cluttered, lockers have items just shoved into them, and even their appearances can look disorganized. Children who are twice-exceptional have twice the reason to be unorganized—their giftedness and their disabilities. Getting twice-exceptional students organized can go a long way in making it easier for them to be able to use their gifts.

Here are some general tips:

» *Set a weekly backpack-cleaning day*: Some students tend to use their backpacks like dumpsters. They put in every piece of paper they receive, carry every book even though it might not be used all week, and have toys and other nonschool necessities. This makes for a very heavy backpack that could end up causing back strain. At least once a week, have students go through and get rid of any material no longer needed. Have conversations about what books are absolutely needed and which ones can go in a locker or be left at home.

» *Make lists of tasks that need to be done*: Lists are just another way to break big jobs into smaller parts. If you give students a multistep assignment, make it manageable by listing steps for students to check off. If a math teacher asks students to work on a set of problems, trade with a partner and grade, and then correct the mistakes, the list might look like this:

> Solve questions 1–9 on page 57.
> Trade with Bobby and grade each other's papers.
> Get your paper back and figure out what mistakes were made.
> Fix your mistakes.

» *Make desk cleaning/organizing a daily routine*: Having a nonfunctional workspace is going to result in work not getting done. The same goes for a student desk. Can he find a pencil when he needs it? Does he have the materials he needs to finish a task? Helping a student clean/organize his desk can be as simple as bringing to his attention that his desk needs some attention. Also important is giving him the time and space to do this.

» *Use graphic organizers*: This is a strategy that teaches twice-exceptional students how to organize their ideas, something they might struggle with using traditional teaching methods. It also serves as a visual reference that allows students to see their thoughts. These students often have difficulty getting ideas from their exceptional brains to the paper. Many graphic organizers can help this process.

» *Show them how to organize a notebook*: As students get older, the need for taking notes will become more prevalent. There are effective ways to organize notes, and there are some that cause confusion. Showing students how to organize their notes can help them review material, study for a test, or write a research paper. How to organize and take notes is addressed in more detail in Cause 7: Lack of Skills.

» *Use a planner*: Human beings forget 90% of what they hear even when they are trying to remember. To help students organize their work and deadlines, a planner is an excellent resource. It can be broken down by subject area, or prioritized by most important to least or by due dates. Learning the value of being organized in their younger years will only translate to good things when students are adults.

» *Color-code entries on calendars*: Some students struggle to write down assignments and thus might not have completed homework that was assigned. When writing assignments on the board, use different colors for different subjects or grades. If you are a teacher who teaches multiple subjects, red might represent language arts while green is social studies. This color-coding is just one more way for you to clearly communicate to students what they are supposed to do.

Teaching students to be organized allows them to learn better, a valuable 21st-century skill.

Strategy 2: Chunking

Some students are very good at seeing the big picture of a long-term assignment. Others, however, especially students with learning disabilities, have difficulty seeing past a day, much less multiple weeks of work. A long-term assignment can be too big a pill to swallow. It needs to be broken into much smaller parts so it can be easily digested.

For instance, if a student is assigned to write a research paper on the effects of gravity, the tasks can be broken down into steps:

1. Research online about gravity.
2. Take notes on what you learn.
3. Go back and indicate where each set of notes fits into the overall outline of the paper.
4. Write these pieces of information on index cards.
5. Organize your index cards.
6. Write a rough draft.
7. Complete a bibliography.
8. Edit rough draft.
9. Type the final draft.
10. Turn it in.

By breaking the assignment into smaller tasks, or chunking, students find it more palatable and can better see how to complete each smaller task. It helps students to see that the project has a beginning, middle, and end. You can also assign deadlines to these tasks so that a student realizes when she is falling behind and needs to increase her efforts to catch up.

One way to help students see this a little better is with a graphic organizer. In this case, an effective graphic organizer might be a calendar (see Table 8). This allows students to visualize how the project is broken up, making it appear more manageable.

Strategy 3: Incorporate a Multisensory Approach

Using two or more senses can increase the amount of learning retention a student has. This would involve incorporating a combination of visuals, sounds, textures, tastes, and smells into the lesson. Using this multisensory approach can help a twice-exceptional student tap into her learning strengths in order to make connections and form memories. It also allows her a wider range of ways to show what she has learned.

TABLE 8

Sample Research Project Calendar

Sunday	Monday	Tuesday	Wednesday	Thursday	Friday	Saturday
	Project assigned.	Research and take notes on gravity.	Research and take notes on gravity.	Research and take notes on gravity.	Research and take notes on gravity.	Organize and label notes.
Organize and label notes.	Write notes on index cards.	Write notes on index cards.	Write notes on index cards.	Organize index cards.	Begin writing rough draft.	Write rough draft.
Write rough draft.	Write rough draft.	Write rough draft.	Complete bibliography.	Edit rough draft.	Edit rough draft.	Type the final paper.
Type the final paper.	Turn in final paper.					

If you are teaching an elementary class about Johnny Appleseed, you could have them watch a video of the Disney song "The Lord is Good to Me," so they are getting visual and auditory learning. Additionally, you could bring in some apples and allow students to smell and taste them. You could conclude by having students plant an apple seed of their own on the school grounds, bringing in tactile and kinesthetic learning.

Figure 10 is an example of a multisensory lesson to teach students about the Constitution. In order to complete the project, students must use a wide variety of senses from visual, auditory, kinesthetic, and tactile learning styles.

Benefits of a multisensory approach include (Hidden Angel Foundation, n.d.):

- » increased concentration and focused attention,
- » heightened awareness and improved alertness,
- » improved coordination and motor development,
- » cognitive development by increased brain function,
- » leading participants to explore their environment,
- » improved creativity,
- » stimulating the sensory building blocks,
- » developing a sense of cause and effect,
- » developing language—more vocalization,
- » promoting social interactions,
- » more calmness and lower aggressive behaviors,
- » increased opportunity for choice and self-determination, and
- » improved communication and sharing (para. 6).

Using this approach with twice-exceptional students allows the disability to be compensated for, while at the same time allowing the child to use his strengths.

Conclusion

Twice-exceptional students can be twice the challenge because their disabilities mask their giftedness or vice versa. The important thing to remember is that this student has gifts that should be focused on.

Schoolhouse Rocks

Remembering the three main principles in the Constitution—federalism, separation of power, and checks and balances—you are going to create a song that teaches an article in the Constitution. Your group will need to:

- Read the article(s) you are assigned.
- Figure out what is important about the article.
- Write a song, either of your own original composition or using music from an already existing song.
- Create a five question, multiple-choice quiz that tests your audience over the information in your song.

Your grade will be based on the following:

1. *Originality/creativity*: How energetic and inventive is your song?
2. *Completeness*: Does your song cover the important parts of the article?
3. *Relevance/quiz*: Are the answers for the quiz covered directly in your song?
4. *Understandability/song sheet*: Can we understand what your group is saying, and is the song sheet legible and correct?

Tips for a better grade:

- You may film your song, but it is not necessary. Video does allow you to do many takes though and use more creative settings.
- Props and costumes always enhance the creativity aspect.
- The chorus should contain the main idea of the article and be repeated at least four times.
- Lyric sheet, quiz, and answer sheet for quiz are due the class before presentation.
- *First and foremost, your song must teach!*

Figure 10. Sample multisensory lesson.

By focusing on these strengths, students can overcome the disability. Finding the correct strategies to tap into these strengths is the key.

If you would like to read more in-depth about one of these strategies or topics, a good resource is *Successful Strategies for Twice-Exceptional Students* by Kevin Besnoy.

Cause 6

LACK OF INTRINSIC MOTIVATION

School is the place we all go to learn, right? Many students see it this way. Others see school as a factory. Its parts and pieces all move in the same manner in order to transport students along a conveyer belt until they receive a piece of paper at the end. The content "taught" at school is not really all that interesting or important in the grand scheme of things. These children may love to learn, but they just do not love to learn what the teacher wants them to. And this just is not underachieving gifted students. Indiana University's High School Survey of Student Engagement polled more than 81,000 students in 110 high schools, across 26 states. The results revealed that 75% thought what was being taught was not interesting (as cited in Bryner, 2007).

Most of us know that sometimes life is not interesting. We have to power through boring meetings, long-winded sermons at church, and dinner with the in-laws, not to mention all of the time sitting in traffic. Most people's jobs are not as interesting as they would like them to be, but they suck it up and persevere because they have to put bread on the table. Would it be great if we found every aspect of our job to be interesting? Would we work harder and produce better results? According to Duckworth (2016), yes. People who like their jobs and find them interesting tend to better do their jobs. The same goes for students. If they find what they are learning in school interesting, they are more motivated to learn. What happens to those students who do not find school interesting? Duckworth found that smarter students actually had less grit than kids who were bright but not considered gifted. This is because bright students compensate by working harder and being more determined; in essence, they are grittier. It is very important to understand the distinction between bright and gifted. A bright student enjoys school. A gifted student enjoys learning (Szabos, 1989). If a gifted student does not feel what is being covered in class is worth his time, he just will not do it. Bright students are almost always motivated by grades—underachieving gifted students not so much.

When Educators Use the L-Word

When a teacher has a student who is gifted but does not want to do the work, she often labels the student as *lazy*. Sure, there are lazy people in the world, but is this student lazy or simply not interested in what is being taught? Oftentimes, lazy is a misdiagnosis. The student is not lazy when it comes to doing things he wants to do. In fact, he works really hard on the things that interest him, such as practicing his guitar for his band, learning how to write code so he can create his own videogame, or becoming obsessed with design after binge-watching a season of *Project Runway*. The problem is he cannot find anything at school to get excited about. This is when students' motivation level goes down. Every teacher's challenge is to keep his or her students engaged.

When Gifted Students Are Not Willing to Play the Game of School

The reality is that school is a game. The earning of grades, completing homework, taking tests, your behavior. All of these are the rules of the game. You have some children who love playing the game of school. For better or worse, these students have success in school. You may have an underachieving gifted student who aces all of the tests but does not turn in any of her homework and receives a C in the class. Then, there is the student who does average on the test but makes sure every piece of homework is turned in, not to mention any extra credit that can be gathered, and earns an A. These students are not being rewarded for their abilities or intelligence. They are being rewarded for playing the game well. For anyone who does not follow the rules of the game, it is really difficult to succeed.

This is not to say the students willing to play the game are in the wrong. They are simply playing the game by the rules they were provided with. You certainly cannot fault them for that. This ability will serve them well when they go to college, and even when they get into the workforce. What employer would not want a worker who does what is asked, shows up to work on time, meets deadlines, works hard, and plays within the rules of the game of work? These workers will probably make it much further than a person who turns out creative and amazing work, but misses deadlines, is not consistent in attendance, only does what is of interest to him, and does not like to play by the rules.

The question is: How do we ensure these unmotivated students get the skills they need to be successful later in life? How do we get someone to win in the game when he or she is not willing to play by the rules? We change the rules to fit the student. Then, the student is able to succeed in the game not by playing by the rules of school, but by finding success by following his or her own rules.

When Gifted Students Lack Goal Valuation

Underachieving gifted students lack goal valuation. This is the degree to which a task is important, interesting, and attainable. For students motivated by school, these three factors are usually present. Even if all three are not felt strongly, one of them is felt so strongly that it compensates for the others. For example, if a student sees what she is doing as very important, she will be motivated to complete it, even if it is not that interesting to her. Or, if she believes it to be highly attainable because other students in the class are doing it as well, and she feels competitive, the lesson will seem important for that very reason.

Students not motivated by school might have difficulty with these factors. They might not find something interesting, so they choose not to do it. Or, if something seems unattainable, they wonder why they should bother trying. If a student feels very strongly against even one of these factors, his motivation is going to be lacking. If for some reason the student is incapable of seeing any of the three, it will be next to impossible to get him motivated to do it.

When Educators Do Not Seek Motivators

Some students may be motivated by being given the responsibility to make choices in what they are going to do in class or by competition. With the underachieving gifted student, the teacher has to find the motivator for that student.

Some teachers might wonder why they have to find the motivation. Should not the student find the motivation for himself? Finding motivation, however, is part of the rules of the game. Remember, these students are not playing the game. Thus, when they are not turning in assignments, what does the teacher do? She penalizes them with a lower grade. But we have already established that these students are not motivated by the prospect of a good grade. Why would they be any more motivated by the threat of a bad grade? As teachers, we believe we are teaching them responsibility and how to be a productive citizen. The thinking is that if students do not learn the lesson now, they will pay for it later on, but if the game of school is not their motivator, how can they possibly learn the lesson? Instead, they become even more disillusioned with school and may end up following the self-fulfilling prophecy the teacher feared. If our goal is to prevent this from happening, then we have to figure out a way to motivate these students.

Practical Solutions

Strategy 1: Independent Research Projects

One method for motivating students is to have them work on independent research projects. Such projects provide the depth students

110

need to be challenged. Many times, the typical classroom lessons are surface level. The educational system practices a mile wide and an inch deep when it comes to teaching standards. Teachers have to cram in so much material over the course of the school year that it can be difficult to cover anything in any depth. What would happen if, instead, teachers taught a standard for a longer period of time and went into greater depth? Would that be a more effective way to learn something than memorizing it? Which do you think is more likely to result in an enduring understanding?

Often, the reason the underachieving gifted student is bored in the classroom is because of this surface-level dusting of education. Let us take teaching the American Revolution as an example. Here are two scenarios:

1. The teacher employs traditional methods of teaching in order to deliver the content. The origins of the war are discussed; there is some reading of primary documents, such as *Common Sense* by Thomas Paine and the Declaration of Independence; the major battles are dissected and debated; the Treaty of Paris is reenacted; and the beginnings of the new nation are touched upon. When this is all finished, the teacher gives a multiple-choice assessment with a couple of essays at the end to add rigor.

2. The teacher begins the unit on the American Revolution. He observes quite quickly that one student already seems to know a lot about what is being discussed. The teacher decides to give this student part of the end-of-unit test at the beginning just to see exactly how much she knows. The student gets a B on the test so the teacher gives her credit for mastering the content tied to the American Revolution. Because of this, instead of going along at the pace of the class and learning content she has demonstrated mastery of, she is offered an in-depth independent research project where she can study a topic of her choice as long as it has something to do with the American Revolution.

Out of these two scenarios, which one is most likely to get a student motivated? If this is an underachieving gifted student who is not inspired by school in the first place, Scenario 2 is going to have the better chance of getting this student motivated. The teacher asks the student if there is anything of particular interest to her concerning the American Revolution. She starts talking about the Boston Massacre and how she wants to learn more about it. The student suggests she do a comparison between the Boston Massacre and the Kent State Massacre. Together, the student and the teacher create some essential questions to guide the independent project.

>> What were the events that led to the Boston Massacre?
>> Who is to blame for the Boston Massacre?
>> What role did propaganda play following the Boston Massacre?
>> How are the Boston Massacre and the Kent State Massacre similar?

In addition, the student would have to come up with a product or products that show what she learned from the project. For example, the student might be a very good artist, so she decides to come up with an analysis for Paul Revere's engraving of the Boston Massacre (see Figure 11). She would discuss the propaganda used in the woodcarving and how it was used to rally support for the colonists against the British. She would then draw two pictures as her product. One picture would display more realistically what the Boston Massacre might have looked like based on her research. The second picture would be a drawing of the Kent State Massacre that would use propaganda in it to take the side of one of the groups involved.

Together, you could also create a rubric to evaluate the project by following these steps:

1. *Create categories*: Break the product down into smaller, more manageable parts. There are times when students will do one part of a project very well, but falter in another aspect. For example, the student might have had excellent information in her project, yet her presentation was not engaging. You want to give credit for the job well done on content but point out how she needs to improve her speaking ability. If there was just an

Figure 11. Paul Revere's Boston Massacre engraving.

overall grade, it might be difficult to see what she did well and still needs to work on. This breaks the grade down into parts so the student can figure out where her specific strengths and weaknesses were located. For example, this student's rubric could assess three categories: (1) her analysis of the Paul Revere engraving, (2) her depiction of the actual Boston Massacre, and (3) her depiction of the Kent State Massacre.

2. *Provide descriptors*: Create descriptions for how each category will be evaluated. Start with the top level (excellent), which the middle (good) and bottom (needs improvement) levels can be formed from. Beginning with the top teaches students to always start with the best, as if that is the expectation. The descriptors for each category at the top level should be a sentence or two and show how the category would look. The more vague a descriptor is, the more difficult it will be to evaluate. For example, an "excellent" descriptor in the "analysis" category

might read: *The Revere engraving is discussed in detail, and the various methods of propaganda are explained, including their bias.*

3. *Tier the descriptors*: Create descriptors for the middle and lower levels in each category. Whatever you put in the top level has to be reflected in the subsequent levels. The easiest way to alter descriptors is using the word *but* for the middle category, and *not* for the lowest category. With the addition of just a few words, the descriptor can go from the excellent to good to needs improvement level.

4. *Check over the rubric*: Have the student look over the rubric to make sure it has met all of the requirements:
    > There are at least three categories with at least three descriptors in each.
    > The same number of descriptors appears in each category.
    > It is legible for the evaluator to use.
    > The descriptors fit into the category. You do not want a content descriptor in organization or a visual in the speaking category.

Once you have the essential questions and rubric, it is up to the student to manage her time. Consider providing her with deadlines and periodic checkpoints to keep her on task. If she consistently shows she is doing the work, you, other than being available as a resource, can leave her to her own devices to carry out the project.

Strategy 2: Mentorships

Another way to get an underachieving gifted student motivated is to connect him with a mentor who has certain skills or knowledge to challenge this student. As teachers, we are often expected to be the expert on our content area. The truth is, we often have to be generalists. We know enough to teach the basics, but there are people who are learning about these topics in such depth that they are experts on very specific parts.

For example, you may have a student in your high school class who has displayed a propensity for engineering. He builds robots on his own time and is fascinated with new technology. As his physics teacher, you have a basic understanding of engineering, but you are not an engineer. How do you challenge this student?

You can contact the local university's engineering department. Many universities have an outreach program for their graduate students, and sometimes professors themselves are willing to take on a student as a mentee. Or, you can contact an organization such as the ACE (architecture, construction, engineering) Mentor Program, which specializes in arranging mentorships between professionals and younger folk, or the National Society of Professional Engineers.

Through a series of phone calls or e-mails, you will be able to find someone who can mentor your student. You can have them begin to communicate by e-mail or even Skype. Then, the student can arrange to visit the engineer in the field. Through this mentorship, the student, on his own time, could work on creating and using solar cells to power an electric wheelchair. This is not for a grade or even tied to the standards of the physics class, but the skills the student is learning are invaluable and will prepare him for what he might face in college or the workforce. As an added bonus, this student might decide to go to school to be an engineer because of his experiences with his mentor, or he might decide engineering is not the right fit for him, which is almost as important.

According to StudentMentor.org (2017), mentorship programs:

> » enhance confidence and challenge students to set higher goals, take risks, and achieve at higher levels;
> » provide recognition, encouragement, and psychosocial support;
> » teach students to balance academic and professional responsibilities;
> » provide role models, a support system, and insiders' perspectives on careers;
> » promote development of interpersonal skills and expose students to diverse perspectives and experiences;
> » offer direct access to powerful resources within students' prospective majors or professions; and

115

» build foundations of lasting professional and personal networks (para. 3).

Strategy 3: Passion Projects

A passion project is just as the title suggests—a student finds a project that motivates him. It might be something he has always wanted to learn about, an extension of something else that interests him, or something suggested by someone else. Passion projects can be set up in a variety of ways. Some classes participate in Genius Hour, "a movement that allows students to explore their own passions and encourages creativity in the classroom" (Genius Hour, 2017, para. 1). Genius Hour provides students with time to work on self-selected projects. Inspired by Google, which allows its engineers to spend 20% of their time to work on any project they want, the idea is simple:

> Allow people to work on something that interests them, and productivity will go up. Google's policy has worked so well that it has been said that 50% of Google's projects have been created during this creative time period. Ever heard of Gmail or Google News? These projects are creations by passionate developers that blossomed from their 20% time projects. (para. 2)

Some teachers use Genius Hour during study halls. Others work it into the regular classroom. Sometimes it is done before or after school. Passion projects are not necessarily tied to curriculum, but they are about learning. Is not that the purpose of school—to learn? By using a passion project with students, you might take an underachieving gifted student and reignite her love for learning that has been quashed by too many years of playing the game of school.

You can do passion projects at any grade level. One of the levels it can be most effective, however, is during senior year. Students in their last semester of school are prone to a "disease" known amongst educators as *senioritis*. A student realizes he is likely to graduate no matter how well or poorly he performs in his final semester. He may already have been accepted to a university or have a job lined up after graduation. So why should he give his best effort in school? Think of the level of attention and focus you get from students in any grade on the last day before the end of the school year. Now imagine that extended over a period of several months. High schools all over the country deal with these uninspired and unmotivated seniors. What if you used a passion project to send them out the door on a positive note? Figure 12 is an example of a project, and Figure 13 shows how the project might be organized.

A passion project such as this will not only work with your underachieving gifted students, but also might help nudge that student who normally would be motivated, but is suffering from a case of senioritis.

Conclusion

Motivating students is a difficult task. Motivating students who are unwilling to play the game of school can be even more of a challenge. The key is to find that spark of love of learning. This can be accomplished by giving students choice in what they are learning. Too many times, students have sat through classes where everyone was given the same material and expected to produce the same cookie cutter assessment. By giving students choice and using teaching strategies such as independent research projects, mentorships, or passion projects, you are allowing them to participate and actually dictate their learning. This might be something that was taken away from them over many years of schooling. Help them to find it again. Help them to discover the learners they are and always will be.

If you would like to read more in-depth about one of these strategies, a good resource is *Genius Hour: Passion Projects That Ignite Innovation and Student Inquiry* by Andi McNair.

The Passion Project

Overview

Students will have 5 weeks to explore a passion of both knowing and doing. The two can be interrelated or having nothing to do with one another. Students will create their own detailed lesson plan for what they will be doing during these 5 weeks, splitting the time between the two objectives as they see fit (i.e., 3 weeks knowing, 2 weeks doing; 2.5 knowing and another 2.5 doing, etc). Students must create authentic performances for each of these objectives to be approved by the teacher.

Essential Questions

1. What is something you have wanted to learn about or know before you graduate from high school that your schooling did not provide?
2. What is something you have always wanted to learn how to do before you go out into the adult world of post-high school?
3. Is there such thing as learning for learning's sake, or does there always have to be a reward for learning?
4. Is it easier to learn something that one is passionate about than something that is chosen for him or her?
5. Does the end of your senior year in high school have to flicker out with a sputter, or can you go out strong with a sense you really learned something valuable at the end?

Schedule

After the first introductory week, students will have for the most part the same schedule for the remaining 5 weeks. It will look something like this:

Monday: Community sharing day—students will sit in community circles and share the progress of their project. There will be no need for a project end presentation to the class because everyone will be sharing their challenges and/or accomplishments to everyone on a weekly basis. The Monday on the final week of class will be spent tying up loose ends and informing the group how each project finished out.

Tuesday, Wednesday, Thursday: Project work days—students will be completing their knowing or doing aspect of the passion project.

Figure 12. Sample passion project.

Friday: Community building days—students and teachers will spend the last month building a deeper sense of community. Two of these Fridays will be literary discussions, but the other three will be activities designed to strengthen our bond with one another.

Products of Project

Lesson Plan/Calendar: On the Monday of the second week, students need to have planned out what they are doing and how it will break down. This will be a detailed plan with an accompanying calendar to show what students will be doing every workday. Students must carefully choose projects that give them enough, but not too much, to do.

Daily Journal: Because students will be working independently Tuesday through Thursday every week, they will be required to write a daily online journal for each of these days. These journal entries will be reporting on the progress of the project and reflections of what was learned.

Authentic Performance: Students will create an authentic performance both for both the knowing and doing aspect of the project. This can be a research paper, presentation, lecture, performance, etc. The performance must be authentic to a real-life audience or can be shown on tape. The authentic performance will be a showing of your accomplishments, not a telling.

Parental Evaluation: Students need to have ongoing discussions about their projects with a parent or guardian. Share with them any products made, successes and challenges you faced, what you learned, and what you plan on doing with regards to the project in the future. Every 2 weeks parents will be required to send an e-mail to reflect on what they have learned from their student about the project.

Literary Discussion: Students will have a few choices here.

1. If students have chosen to read a book or books as part of their knowing aspect of the project, they will share this in the literary discussions.
2. If students have a book they have always wanted to read or neglected to read and want to before graduating, they may chose this to read for their literary guild.
3. If students have a particular book they have read and want to share with others, they may bring it in and recommend it to classmates.

The end result is that everyone will be reading a book of their choice or that was recommended to them, and we will have literary discussions in small groups the third and fifth Friday of the project.

Figure 12. *Continued.*

119

Monday	Tuesday	Wednesday	Thursday	Friday
1 Introduction of Passion Project	2 Guest speakers on the passions of knowing and doing	3 Advisory day with teacher	4 Advisory day with teacher/book exchange	5 Have Passions Projects selected
6 Turn in lesson plan and calendar for Passion Project	7 Work day; Online journal due	8 Work day; Online journal due	9 Work day; Online journal due	10 Community Building Day; First Parent Reflection due
11 Community Sharing Day	12 Work day; Online journal due	13 Work day; Online journal due	14 Work day; Online journal due	15 First Literary Discussion
16 Community Sharing Day	17 Work day; Online journal due	18 Work day; Online journal due	19 Work day; Online journal due	20 Community Building Day; Second Parent Reflection due
21 Community Sharing Day	22 Work day; Online journal due	23 Work day; Online journal due	24 Work day; Online journal due	25 First Literary Discussion
26 Community Sharing Day	27 Authentic Performance Day	28 Authentic Performance Day	29 Authentic Performance Day	30 Final Community Building Day; Final Reflection

Figure 13. Sample passion project calendar.

Cause 7

LACK OF SKILLS

There are misconceptions about gifted students. Many think that if students are gifted, they can automatically take good notes, know how to study for tests, or write in complete sentences. These assumptions cause a lot of gifted students to find themselves in a place where they do not have the skills to be successful. Skills are much different than ability. A student may be gifted in math, so he has the ability to answer complex problems. He might not, however, be able to explain to others how he got his answer.

People often say that the best athletes are not necessarily the best coaches of their sport. For example, Ken Griffey, Jr., was once the best player in baseball, as evidenced by winning the league's MVP in 1997. He possessed a very natural swing and was a five-tool player, meaning he had speed and could catch, throw, hit for average, and hit for power. These sorts of players are very rare, which is part of the reason Griffey was enshrined into the Hall of Fame in 2016. But would Griffey make a very good coach? Probably not. Griffey possessed natural talent. You cannot teach speed. You cannot learn strength. You either have superb hand-eye coordination or you do not. These things came naturally to him. Because of this, it may be difficult for him to put into words how he does what he does. It just comes to him from his talent. The same can be said about many gifted students. You cannot teach someone to be gifted. These students just have the natural ability to look at something from another perspective or see a pattern others do not. This is not something they have developed; it is something they were born with. A lot of times, answers come easily to them, but they cannot necessarily explain them. As a result, getting gifted students to show their work in math or to write a detailed response in English language arts can be a challenge. This gap between ability and skills can cause a gifted student to start to fall behind—and begin to underachieve.

When Answers Come Easily to Gifted Students

In their younger years, gifted students stick out a lot more. If you were to have someone observe an elementary classroom that had one gifted student, it probably would not take very long for this person to be able to spot which kid it is. If you put that same person in a high school classroom with the same mission, however, it is probably going to be more difficult to discern. Why?

Students considered gifted in the lower grades usually have a lot of content knowledge that their age-mates do not possess. This is part of what identifies them as gifted. A student who has been reading since she was 3 is going to be ahead of the other first graders who maybe did not learn to read until they were 6. Or a student whose parents took him to the conservatory every week might have a better grasp on science than the student who has never been. There are clear gaps between these students due to different experiences. Although it is impossible to fill in all the gaps, once students are in school for several years, others may begin to catch up with those who came in with the advantage. Suddenly a wide gap between students is either closed or much smaller.

Not only that, as the students move up in grade levels, the schoolwork becomes much more difficult. This is a natural progression as students are introduced to new content they have not been exposed to before. There are not many chances in everyday life to be exposed to quantum physics or algebraic notation. At this point in their school careers, things have always come easy to them and they have not had to work as hard as age-mates in order to produce quality work. They do not have the skillset to learn new material or push past a challenge. When students have faced challenges their entire school careers and are faced with another, they have coping skills to get past it. If a student has never had a challenge until he gets into middle school, the obstacle may prove to be immovable. Rather than tackling it, these types of students stop in their tracks. This is when underachievement can set in.

When the Focus Is on Memorization, Not 21st-Century Survival Skills

Students often must employ lower level thinking skills in order to be successful. Most states employ content standards, which teachers are responsible for teaching to their students, leading to state assessments. How many of these state assessments are asking higher level questions that dig deep into the learning that has occurred? Considering these assessments are mostly multiple choice, not many. In order to prepare students for these high-stakes tests, teachers resort to teaching a lot of facts, but do not go into much depth.

If a classroom requires a lot of rote memorization, or completing and turning something in gets students full credit, the gifted student is not going to be able to access the depths of his talents. If the gifted student gets bored, he may even elect not to complete assignments or turn them in, causing underachievement. A mediocre student, on the other hand, could be very successful accessing the lower levels of Bloom's taxonomy (see p. 153 for more about this concept) and working hard. The compliant student is going to find much more success in this setting than a student who is itching to be challenged.

This is not to suggest that the standards should not be taught, but the method in which these standards are taught needs to be more than just surface level. You need to allow students to learn valuable skills, skills that they will be able to use later in life, as well as the content. The problem with the focus on content is that many students will never use it again. Are you computing geometry in your everyday life, have you ever had to recite the Gettysburg Address, or have you ever in a job interview been asked to provide an analysis of *The Great Gatsby*? Probably not. But there are 21st-century survival skills we could instill, while teaching the content, including (Trilling & Fadel, 2009):

1. accessing and analyzing information,

2. curiosity and imagination,
3. initiative and entrepreneurialism,
4. adaptability,
5. effective oral and written communication,
6. critical thinking and problem solving, and
7. collaboration across networks (p. xxvi).

If you were a prospective employer looking at applicants' skills, you would want to hire the person with these skills on the spot.

How difficult would it be to have students working on something where they are learning one or maybe more of these survival skills, mastering the content at the same time? Take, for example, the social studies project in Figure 14. Students might learn a lot of facts about the Renaissance and be able to take it a step further and see connections between the accomplishments of that time and what they led to. More importantly, however, they are going to have to learn and employ the following 21st-century survival skills (Trilling & Fadel, 2009):

>> accessing and analyzing information—when researching their choices;
>> curiosity and imagination—when creating their structure in the bonus opportunity;
>> effective oral and written communication—in the presentation where they convince the class of their choice;
>> critical thinking and problem solving—determining which ideas are more important than others; and
>> collaboration across networks—working as a group on the project (p. xxvi).

These are all skills they can use in any class, including science, health, or even home economics. Information about the Renaissance will not come in handy as much in those classes, but the skills learned will continue to be useful. If you are going to buy a car, you would want to analyze information about what sort of car is best for you. You would have to have effective oral communication skills to broker a deal with the salesman. You might have to employ critical thinking in order to see how it might fit in your budget or what upgrades would be affordable

---

Renaissance Hall of Fame

There are all sorts of hall of fames, whether for sports, music, motorcycles, inventions, etc. You have been charged with creating a hall of fame that represents the Renaissance. Your group will choose 10 ideas from the Renaissance that will be inducted into the hall of fame. Decisions you will have to make:

- What makes it in? What doesn't?
- What scientific, cultural, or social changes did each idea lead to?
- Why have you made the choices you have?

You will present these decisions to the class for consideration. You must also create an exhibition for the top 3 ideas and how they will be displayed in the hall of fame.

You will be graded on the following three criteria:

- Presentation
- Content
- Display

Bonus Opportunity: Design the building/make a model of where the Hall of Fame will be housed based on Renaissance architecture and/or influence of other Renaissance ideas.

Figure 14. Sample social studies project.

---

and practical. Collaboration might come in handy when working with the financial person, the service person, and other people involved in the buying and selling of the car.

Teaching students valuable skills on top of the content they are required to know will go a long way in equipping them to succeed in learning and in life.

Practical Solutions

Strategy 1: Test-Taking Skills

If you are teaching sixth graders, you might assume students coming to you would have at least seven years of test-taking skills. This would be a poor assumption to make. You would be better to assume that students do not know how to properly take a test and to provide them with these skills. What you do not want is a student missing a question because he does not have the test-taking skills. If a student misses a question, you want it to be because he has not mastered the content.

Here is an example of how an English teacher might train her students how to write an essay:

- » Read the question first.
  - › Number the parts.
  - › Underline key phases.
  - › Make sure you understand what it is asking.

- » Think before you write.
  - › Organize your notes and thoughts.
  - › Don't simply copy your notes.
  - › Get an idea of what you want to answer and find what you need to do so.
  - › Don't start until you are ready to answer.

- » Be clear in your explanation.
  - › Is it detailed enough that it is clear to someone else reading it?
  - › Ask "Why?" at the end of each statement.
  - › Would someone who knows nothing about the topic understand it the way you explained it?

- » Use evidence to back up your statements.
  - › Three examples are always good to show understanding.
  - › Remember to include important terms.
  - › Make sure you explain the examples clearly and how they fit with your statement.

- » Remember to answer the question (ATQ).
  - › Reread the question and reread the answer.
  - › Do they make sense together?
  - › Don't include items that don't ATQ.

By introducing these guidelines at the beginning of the school year, students will clearly understand expectations and learn skills that will benefit them in any essay they write.

This goes for any type of test you give in your classroom. Are students properly trained on how to take that format of test? Even if you have multiple-choice tests and in your directions you say, "Make sure you read all of the questions before answering any of them," your last question could read, "Leave this test blank with the exception of your name for full credit. Any erasure marks will result in a zero." Although some students might feel they are being tricked, it is just a method of getting them to slow down and take their time on the test. Are students knowledgeable about how to eliminate distractors and use process of elimination to find the correct answer?

If students take a majority of their end-of-year exams on a computer, are they comfortable with using this format? Do you need to create tests of your own that use this model so that students can develop confidence in using it?

Strategy 2: Study Skills

When a test is coming up, teachers often assign studying as homework. But have students ever been shown how to study? Gifted students might be able to wing some tests using their keen common sense and critical thinking skills, but sooner or later, whether in junior high, high school, college, or the bar exam, they will come across a test they need to study for in order to succeed. Have your students been given the necessary tools in order to study effectively?

Students need to find the right study strategies for them. Here are some examples to share with students:

1. *Rewrite information in your own words*: Try to rewrite what you have learned so that it makes sense to you. Recopy notes, put the essential question in your own words, or summarize the main lesson that was emphasized. You can even elaborate on what was written, providing more of an understanding.

2. *Use mnemonic devices*: These are triggers used to remember pieces of information using an association. For example, you

can learn the cardinal directions using "Never Eat Soggy Waffles," or use "HOMES" to remember the Great Lakes of Huron, Ontario, Michigan, Erie, and Superior.

3. *Practice with friends or family*: Have someone quiz you. Have a friend or family member review your notes and formulate questions from them or test you on essential vocabulary.

4. *SQ3R method*: This strategy will help you think about a text (Robinson, 1970):
    > *Survey*: Get the general idea of the reading.
    > *Question*: Write down questions that you have from the reading.
    > *Read*: Look for the answers to the questions you have posed.
    > *Recite*: Say the answers to the questions and quiz yourself on your comprehension of them.
    > *Review*: Go over your answers and see if you have any unanswered questions.

5. *Use notecards or flashcards*: A memory retention strategy that focuses the attention on key points helps both auditory and visual learners. By saying words aloud you are hearing them, and by reading you are seeing them. This causes the information to transform from short- to long-term memories.

6. *Practice time management*: Cramming just hours before your test might allow you to learn the information in the short term, but will not help you to understand it. If you know your test is a week away, do not wait until the last minute to study. Spaced repetition is one such strategy. It involves spreading out the studying over a period of time, increasing the amount of time with each session. The first time you might sit down and study for 15 minutes. The next time could be half an hour. Eventually you would work up to even longer stretches of time, such as an hour. You do this over the course of a week rather than trying to cram in a 4-hour session all in one evening when most of what you have studied will be forgotten.

7. *OK4R method*: This method allows you to comprehend and retain information (Levy, 2011):
    > *Overview*: Get an idea of what the text is about.
    > *Key ideas*: Decide what needs to be learned.
    > *Read*: Read the text from beginning to end.
    > *Recall*: Put the text away and try to remember the key points.
    > *Reflect*: Reflect on the previous steps to keep the information in your memory.
    > *Review*: At a later time, go over the text again to trigger your memory.

8. *Overlearn*: Manipulate the material in as many ways as possible, such as writing, reading, touching, hearing, and saying it. Review the information in multiple ways to increase your chances of retaining it.

9. *Frequently review material*: If you do not review material, you can forget 80% of what you learned. Even before you have a test coming up, review what you have read, your notes, or your assignments as often as possible. The first review should come the same day or the day after you learned it. By reviewing often, studying for the test will not be as daunting.

10. *Chunk material*: Organize information into groups. You can chunk material in different ways depending on what you are trying to learn. If you have 10 terms to learn, you can group them into two groups of five to make it more manageable. Finding patterns in information is another way. This can be mnemonic, or it could be sequential. Remembering the pattern will trigger your memory of the individual pieces. A final way to chunk information is through organizing it by an essential question or theme. By finding the information that fits into a theme, you can organize it and make it easier to recall.

Strategy 3: Note-Taking Skills

Note-taking is a very important skill. Without it, when you go to study, you are working with incomplete or incorrect material. Teaching a student to take good notes need not wait until junior high or high school. As early as elementary school, a student can be exposed to strategies for taking notes.

Good notes require taking large amounts of information and recording them in a much more succinct manner. Notes should not be a transcript of what was said, but a summation of the main points. Note-takers do not need to worry about writing conventions, such as complete sentences, punctuation, spelling, or other grammar. The idea is to capture the main idea in as short a sentence as possible. Think of Tarzan. When Tarzan introduces himself, he does not worry about formality. He would not say, "Allow me to introduce myself. My name is Tarzan." He would say, "Me Tarzan." Each says the same thing; one is just more concise. The same thing goes with notes. If the information you have been given is, "With the Louisiana Purchase in 1803, the United States purchased approximately 828,000,000 square miles of territory from France, thereby doubling the size of the young republic," then with some creative note-taking, this mouthful could become the much shorter: "Louisiana Purchase (1803), 828 thou. sq. mi, doubled U.S."

Here are some overall tips for students to use when writing notes:

>> Don't use complete sentences—think in Tarzan talk. Eliminate articles (the, a, of), and don't worry about correct punctuation or spelling.

>> Use abbreviations (e.g., Native Americans = NA, United States = U.S., environment = env.).

>> Use symbols and Twitter talk (e.g., definition (=); and/or (&, /); BTW, B4, NBD, TL).

>> Combine sentences and information.

>> Organization is essential. Don't cram notes into a single paragraph. Use a system that allows the notes to flow and makes it easy to find information.

There is no right or wrong way to take notes, but organization is really important. Here are a few examples of methods to share with students:

1. *The Cornell method*: Divide the paper into two columns—a smaller column on the left and a wider one on the right. The larger column should be used as the main area to take notes. For each new topic, the notetaker should skip a couple of lines to indicate a new topic. Use the column on the left to place important phrases and terms that would cause the reader to remember the more detailed information (see Figure 15). This is a good method for notes you are taking for information needed for a test. The keywords and phrases in the left-hand column act as a trigger for knowing the more detailed information you will need for the test. It does require some organization skills and possibly summarizing notes after the class is over.

2. *The outlining method*: This involves using a system of dashes or indented outlining. Begin at the left with a main topic. With each piece of information related to the main topic, you indent to the right (see Figure 16). When a new topic is introduced, you go back to the left margin. This is a useful method because notes can be written in short spurts linked together by the overall main topic. Also, most speakers give their information in an outline format.

3. *The mapping method*: This method involves drawing blocks or circles of information and then mapping evidence and supporting in connected boxes or circles. The middle bubble or block has the main point and anything connected to it are subtopics or pieces of evidence or support. This is a very visual style that takes up a lot of space, but it is helpful to those who like to draw (see Figure 17).

Often, the information students receive is being spoken to them in either a lecture or oral lesson. This requires that the student listens and captures the main information. Share with students some things to listen for when taking notes:

» If something is repeated several times, it is important.

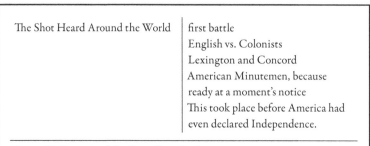

The Shot Heard Around the World	first battle
	English vs. Colonists
	Lexington and Concord
	American Minutemen, because ready at a moment's notice
	This took place before America had even declared Independence.

Figure 15. Example of the Cornell method.

I. Old North Bridge
   a. Stopped British
      i. 400 men turning away nearly 100 British troops
   b. Sign that Colonists were not going to be pushed around
II. Lexington

Figure 16. Example of the outlining method.

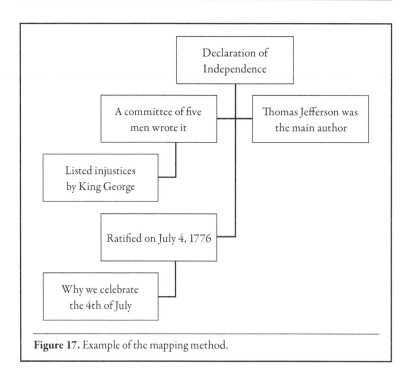

Figure 17. Example of the mapping method.

> » If the teacher is using a PowerPoint, look for things that are underlined, *italicized*, or in **bold**.
> » If something goes on for more than two slides, it is important.
> » Listen for things such as "the most significant thing was" or "the primary effect was" or "what is unique about this is."
> » Look for themes.
> » Don't write down all examples (3–4 will do) but try to write down ones you will recall later.
> » When given a numbered list, write it down.
> » If something is spelled out for you, it is probably important.
> » Make sure you know the answer to the essential question.
> » Look at the big picture.

Strategy 4: Research Skills

Another extremely important skill is the ability to research. This is the first of the 21st-century survival skills: accessing and analyzing information. With the advent of the Internet, information is a mere mouse click away. No longer do students need to toil in libraries, culling books in order to find the information they need, when a simple Google search will provide a million websites full of information. Although having a million places to find information is nice, knowing how to navigate and locate the one that is best going to help you is an important skill to possess. Figure 18 is an example of research tips to share with students. By learning how to conduct research properly, students can find out anything for themselves. This is a skill than can be used in any class as well as in their lives.

Conclusion

Do not assume that just because a student is gifted she possesses the skills needed in order to be successful in the classroom. Many times, because answers used to come easily to her or she was able to get by on her intelligence, she never had to learn the skills until she was far enough into her educational career that underachievement began to

---

How to Research

You can find almost anything on the Internet, which means you always have to go through a lot of things that might not be relevant to your topic. There are various search engines to help them you information, such as:

- Google (http://www.google.com),
- Yahoo (http://www.yahoo.com), and
- Bing (http://www.bing.com).

When you search, you will want to:

- be as specific as possible without being too specific (e.g., too general = "airplanes," too specific = "paper airplanes with cool decals");
- narrow your search without eliminating sites because they do not contain the exact wording; and
- not just use the first website you encounter (i.e., just because it comes up in a search does not mean it is what you are looking for).

Imagine your teacher has instructed you to create a report. You decide that your report will be about hippos. If you do a random search on Google using the keyword *hippos*, your search would retrieve more than 16 million results. That's more than you, or anyone, can possibly go through. How do you refine your search?

Step 1: Construct Research Questions

Write specific questions. Doing so will help you narrow your topic and determine exactly what information you need. Sample questions:

- What sort of animal is a hippo?
- Where do hippos commonly live?
- What do hippos like to eat?
- How many hippos are there in the world?
- What is the oldest known fossil record of hippos?
- How many people are attacked by hippos in a year?

Step 2: Figure Out Possible Sources of Information

Before going online, try to identify any sources that might have information on your topic. For example, you might list:

Figure 18. Sample student research skills handout. Adapted from *10 Performance-Based Projects for the Language Arts Classroom: Grades 3–5* (pp. 99, 102–103), by T. Stanley, 2017, New York, NY: Routledge Copyright 2017 by Taylor & Francis. Adapted with permission.

- National Geographic
- African Wildlife Foundation
- Any zoos such as the San Diego, St. Louis, or Philadelphia
- Videos of hippos on sites such as YouTube, Discovery Channel, or Animal Planet

Step 3: Identify Keywords

Review the questions and sources you brainstormed in Steps 1–2, and circle the keywords. What is it specifically you want to find? Use this to refine your search.

Step 4: Get Ready to Search

You are finally ready to choose a tool(s) and begin your search. Depending on the time you have and your own personal preference, you can start with a search engine or a specific site of your own choice.

If you are using a search engine, you will want to use the keywords you identified in Step 3 to develop your search query. The trick is to try several combinations of keywords. Remember—there's no one *right* way to conduct research online. Just be sure to start with a strategy and experiment with different search tools to get the best results.

Step 5: Finding Easy-to-Understand, School-Appropriate Sites

Adding a simple suffix to your search may result in more student-appropriate, student-friendly results. For instance, refine your search to add the following:

- ... for kids
- ... for students
- ... for children
- ... for school

These will make the hits you receive from your search more age-appropriate and easy to understand because you will be the audience they are written for.

Figure 18. *Continued.*

creep in. The four skills that would benefit students in school as well as come in handy in the real world would be test-taking skills, study skills, note-taking skills, and research skills. These 21st-century survival skills will enable students to be successful in any setting, school or otherwise.

If you would like to read more in-depth about one of these strategies, a good resource is the 10 Performance-Based Projects series by Todd Stanley.

Cause 8

LACK OF PROGRAMMING OR TRAINED TEACHERS

All schools are not created equal when it comes to gifted programming. Local schools are given an immense amount of latitude to work with in regard to what gifted programming, if any, they offer. Unlike with special education students, who are protected under federal law by the Individuals with Disabilities Education Act (IDEA, 1990), there is no law stating that students must be provided with gifted programming. The question remains, what do we do for underachieving gifted students, and how do we, as an educational system, challenge them? An easy fix would be just to add more services. After all, these are potentially our future doctors, lawyers, politicians, and other such citizens who will be a major factor in steering our society into the future. Would we not want them to have the very best education possible to make these paths easier to traverse?

Yet, very few dollars are devoted to these bright students: For every $100 our federal government spends on education, $3 goes to gifted programming; $91 goes to programs for struggling students. That means if the federal government gave a district $1,000, they would have enough money for gifted to purchase a single $30 textbook. For a classroom set of textbooks for gifted students, the federal government would have to provide $30,000. Very little of a school's funding comes from the federal government, however. It would probably be more indicative to look at how much the states are spending on gifted programming because this is where a good bulk of school funding comes from. Nearly 40% of districts with elementary gifted programs, 51% of the districts with middle school programs, and 60% of high schools, receive no gifted funding (Callahan, Moon, & Oh, 2014).

Each state decides for itself whether it is going to mandate programming and fund it or not. It looks something like Figure 19. States in green have gifted services that are mandated and fully funded by the state. That is only four states out of 50 that value the education of high-ability students enough to fully pay for it. The purple states mandate gifted programming but are only partially funded by the state. Orange states have gifted services mandated, but the state provides no funds to run the programming. Yellow states do not mandate gifted programming, but state funding is available for those who choose to provide it. The red states mandate no gifted programming and offer no gifted funds.

Although most states have laws that require districts to provide testing for giftedness of their student population, when and how often this testing occurs is left up to the district to determine.

A district might test for giftedness for science in the fifth grade but then never provide the opportunity again. That means the student has a single chance to be identified as gifted in that area. There are other schools that test for giftedness multiple times every year using a test like MAP (Measures of Academic Progress), which gives students multiple chances to be identified in reading and math. It is important to find out the gifted testing policy of your school district and when and how often it tests for giftedness. The district also might have retesting opportunities upon request.

When There's No Gifted Programming

Because a district has the autonomy to make decisions about how it offers gifted services, there are some districts that do not have any gifted programming whatsoever. This is either because the gifted population is not large enough to warrant a full class of services, budgetary reasons cause the district to focus resources elsewhere, or the district

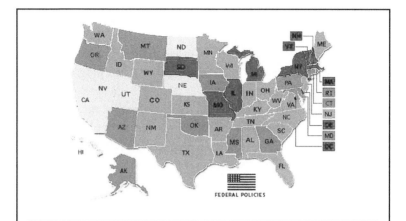

Figure 19. Gifted programming in each state. From "What's New in Gifted Education," by Davidson Institute for Talent Development, 2009, retrieved from http://news.ditd.org/June_09/eNews_June_09_web.htm. Copyright 2009 by Davidson Institute for Talent Development, http://www.davidsongifted.org. Reprinted with permission.

feels it meets the special needs of these students with high expectations in its regular classrooms. Several longitudinal studies have shown the positive effect gifted programs have on students' post-secondary plans. One study (Lubinski et al., 2001) found that 320 gifted students identified during adolescence, who were involved in gifted programming through the secondary level, pursued doctoral degrees at more than 50 times the base rate expectations. When the researchers checked in with these students at the age of 38, 63% reported holding master's degrees and above. Of these, 44% held doctoral degrees. Only around 2% of the general population held a doctoral degree, according to the 2010 U.S. Census (Kell, Lubinski, & Benbow, 2013).

Regardless of its importance, if a school is not willing to provide specific programming for its gifted student population, what it cannot take away is good teaching. If you have teachers who are willing to challenge students and provide them with the education needed to grow, then a lack of programming is not the end of the world. You just need to figure out what strategies work with these students.

When There's No Proper Gifted Programming

Even if a district does have gifted programming, is it effective gifted programming? What constitutes high-quality gifted programming is debatable. Ideally, the best solution is offering a magnet program where students are exposed to a robust and rigorous curriculum, designed to challenge high-ability thinkers, that is provided by teachers who have gone through the gifted certification process. With the additional bussing as well as the teacher training, this could be somewhat expensive for a school system. There are certainly more economical ways to offer gifted programming.

Some choose to cluster gifted students so they are with a few peer-mates who act and think similarly to them. This works if you have a decent-sized gifted population to pull from, but if not, this can be a challenge. Others differentiate in the regular classroom. The idea is to meet the individual student where he is performing. This means if a gifted student is advancing quicker than the rest of the class, the teacher designs lessons to meet these needs. Although this is nice in theory, doing this in a class that has a wide range of abilities can be daunting. Teachers are pulled in other directions by special education students, English language learners, and other groups that might need more time to grasp a concept, pulling them away from the gifted students who need less time. And sometimes differentiation is done in a rigid fashion. Consider reading groups. Do you put the students in the same groups all the time, or do you group them according to how they pretested? Flexible grouping is the key to differentiation, and it takes a lot of work.

Sometimes the service does not match the need. For example, if you have 15 gifted students identified as gifted in math and 32 identified as gifted in reading, yet the program you offer is a math pull-out, you are leaving 32 students without service. It would be better if the program offered reading pull-out to meet the need of a greater number of students. Science and social studies often receive the short end of the stick when it comes to gifted programming. There are not many programs specific to these subject areas, meaning that students who are identified are not going to have their needs met.

Some schools like to claim service through rigorous programs such as Advanced Placement, College Credit Plus, or International Baccalaureate. Although these programs are certainly more challenging in regard to content, they are not specifically designed to meet the unique needs of gifted students. Although instructors might have received specialized training in how to deliver the content of the class, they are not given training in how to challenge gifted students.

When Teachers Do Not Have Skills to Teach Gifted Students

In some cases, teachers working with the gifted population might not have received any training in working with gifted students. We all like to think that good teaching is good teaching, so it should not matter what students a teacher is working with. If she is a good teacher, she will get good results. The reality is that certain types of teachers work well with certain types of students. A teacher who has had a lot of success with special education students might have the innate ability to break things down into smaller parts to make them easier. If you were to put this teacher with a gifted population, the skills might not match up. Gifted students need a teacher who can think quickly on his feet in order to ask higher level questions and encourage critical thinking. This sort of teacher might confuse average students, however, who are not ready to be pushed to think more deeply about a concept or who need more supports before getting to that level.

It is also up to the individual district to decide how it will offer professional development to teachers working with the gifted population. Some districts offer an extensive amount of professional development, exposing teachers to the latest teaching strategies that work well with gifted students. They support teachers going to gifted conferences such as the National Association for Gifted Children's annual convention, offer waivers for classes at the university that are designed to provide gifted instruction, make available online modules, webinars, or trainings, and have in-house professional development, such as book studies, teacher-based teams, or yearlong discussions. These are all methods that will ensure that the teacher who is providing service to the gifted students is prepared to do so.

Some districts have coordinators who coach teachers to work with gifted students and meet with parents to make sure their child is being challenged. Other districts choose not to offer anything in the way of professional development. There are districts that farm out the gifted coordinator position to someone handling many districts, or an administrator with many other duties, meaning this person has just enough time to make sure the district is following the state mandates for identification and service with no additional time to work with teachers.

It is important to have the right people in place to work with the gifted students along with the proper supports and resources in place. If this is not the case, this mismatch could result in gifted students not having their needs met and thus becoming underachievers.

Practical Solutions

Strategy 1: Learning Centers

A learning center is an independent space set up inside the classroom to provide engaging lessons that enrich student learning. This is why it is an especially effective teaching strategy with gifted students. You can set up your learning centers to extend content already learned, allowing students to go deeper. There are various resources at these centers that allow the students to complete their task. Learning centers also give students the opportunity to have hands-on learning experiences.

Consider a teacher who is covering a unit on landforms. She has set up learning centers all around the room, each one covering a different type of landform. You might have volcanoes, mountains, valleys, islands, and deserts. A student could sit down at the learning center for volcanoes and learn about how volcanoes form, what causes them to erupt, and some of the most famous volcanoes. This could be displayed on a trifold, earmarked in a book, a video on the computer, or an actual model of the volcano. Students would complete the task the learning center has asked of them, learning about the topic in the process.

The great thing about learning centers is you can use them to differentiate as well. You might have three different learning centers covering the topic of volcanoes. One of these centers gives you the very basics of volcanoes, the information every student should know. Another one would go a little deeper, asking students to create rather than just comprehend the knowledge. The third one would pose questions designed to make students think about this basic information at a high level, such as predicting when a volcano is going to erupt or what might have happened had volcanoes not formed in the South Pacific. Students would go to the learning center that indicates their prior knowledge of the topic. If a student knows all the basics, she might want to start at the third learning center. If a student knows nothing, he would want to start at the first one.

How you set up learning centers is completely up to you, but Figure 20 shows a basic format.

A learning center is like having an additional teacher in the classroom. It acts as a resource that can enrich the student by reinforcing what has been taught and extending the learning.

There are several choices a teacher can make when it comes to learning centers. They can be used as a rotational system where students work independently, or they can work in small groups. Students can select the learning center they want to be at or the teacher can assign it. The amount of time a student is to spend at a center can vary, as can the implementation. Even with all of these choices, there are a few things that learning centers should include, according to Manzone (2014):

> » *Location*: Learning centers should have a designated spot in the classroom away from the regular lesson so that students can work in a self-directed environment.
> » *Title*: Learning centers should have a label making it very clear what the focus is. It could be something content-specific such as *antonyms* or more thematic such as *revolution*.
> » *Task cards*: Each learning center needs to have clear directions written on task cards so that students know exactly what they

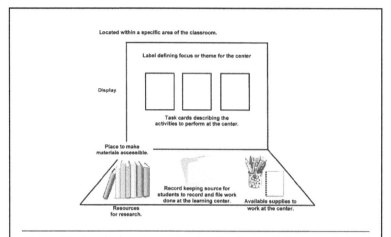

Located within a specific area of the classroom.

Label defining focus or theme for the center

Display

Task cards describing the activities to perform at the center.

Place to make materials accessible.

Record keeping source for students to record and file work done at the learning center.

Resources for research.

Available supplies to work at the center.

Figure 20. Sample learning center format. Designed for a professional development workshop based on Project Linking Learning (2009–2012), Dr. Sandra K. Kaplan, funded by the Jacob K. Javits Gifted and Talented Student Education Act. Reprinted with permission of Jessica Manzone, University of Southern California.

need to do. Task cards can even be differentiated for different learning levels.

» *Time frame*: Learning centers need to allow students enough time to accomplish all of the tasks while not becoming repetitive. You should encourage students to develop time management skills as part of their self-directedness, but some guidance is still helpful.

» *Resources and supplies*: Make sure you provide students with the materials needed to complete their tasks. If you are asking them to be artistic, include art supplies. If you are asking them to research, there should be books or access to the Internet. The students should not have to go outside of the learning center in order to accomplish their tasks.

» *Recording system*: With so much independent work going on, you need to have a system to track the work students are doing. This can be something as simple as a sign-in log, to portfolios of work, to individual journals.

» *Management strategy*: Even though the students are self-directed, you need to figure out how best to direct students in the management of the learning centers. How many students can be at the center at a time? How are groups going to be set up? How do students know to rotate to another learning center? Students should be familiar with this so they do not become confused (para. 3–9).

By having these elements in your learning centers, you will be able to produce a well-oiled machine of classroom management where students know what the expectations are. The most important benefit to using learning centers is that they teach many, if not all, of the 21st-century survival skills discussed previously. If your school does not have gifted programming, learning centers are a good way to challenge gifted students in the regular classroom as well as differentiate for high-ability thinkers.

Strategy 2: Blended Learning

Blended learning is one of those buzzwords popular amongst educational innovators. With the increase in technology in the world, increasing the amount of technology we use in the classroom makes perfect sense. But what does blended learning look like? Do we put a computer into the hands of a student and expect it to teach them? Like any other teaching resource, you need to find a way to use technology as enrichment for a particular lesson. If you can teach the lesson better without the technology, you should not be using it. Technology for technology's sake is a poor model for use in the classroom.

How does one use blended learning in a classroom with gifted students? There are six models to consider when using blended learning (Thompson, 2016):

» *Face-to-face*: For a diverse classroom with high-ability and below-average students, this model allows gifted students to move forward at a more rapid pace. The teacher drives students' progress, in some cases giving them the websites to go to, and monitors their progress. It does allow for differentiation but is not as self-directed as other models.

» *Rotation*: Students rotate through stations, each of which includes technology. There is a combination of face-to-face time with the teacher and online work. Students can be divided into groups based on skill level. Those struggling will get more face-to-face time.

» *Flex*: The teacher acts as a facilitator, but most instruction is online. Although this can be used with gifted students to allow them to work at their own pace, the online content usually is not very in-depth.

» *Online lab*: The instruction is completely online. There are not certified teachers present but paraprofessionals who supervise. Many community and credit recovery schools use this model. It is not ideal for gifted learners, but works for those who may need flexibility with their schedule because of other responsibilities. It does allow gifted students to progress faster than a traditional school setting but does not necessarily provide the amount of depth to challenge them.

» *Self-blend*: Traditional class time provides the basic instruction, and online content is used to supplement. This model is useful if a student exhausts all of the traditional classes a school has to offer and wants additional learning. Students can use this method to take college courses for credit without having to leave the school. This works fairly well with gifted students because it allows them to be independent learners. It also works well with underachieving gifted students who are turned off by traditional schooling and need an alternative to motivate them.

» *Online driver*: There is little to no interaction face-to-face with the teacher. Students work from home, and any questions are communicated electronically with the instructor. This can work with gifted students who are highly motivated and want to move much faster than a traditional school setting allows.

Matching the correct model with the needs of students is important. If a student has been in the system long enough and has turned his back on traditional education, nontraditional methods such as online school lab and online driver might be more appropriate. If the underachieving gifted student is just at the beginning of her disillusionment, having interactive models such as the face-to-face and station rotation to reengage her in school would be beneficial.

Strategy 3: Students as Teacher

The National Training Laboratories (NTL) in Bethel, ME, conducted a study to determine what type of learning caused students to retain information best. The NTL looked at different intelligences such as listening and seeing, as well as different methods of learning. What they found was that the most effective learning, where students retain 90% or more of what they learn, is to teach others. Now this is different than putting a gifted child with someone who is having difficulty and expecting him or her to tutor the child to success. This is about gifted students sharing what they have learned on their terms and being able to communicate this clearly to others. And yet, we rarely use this learning style in the classroom. A traditional classroom will probably have activities such as lecture, reading, and audiovisual components, which when added together only give a 60% retention rate (see Figure 21).

As teachers, we have to become experts on the content before we can teach it to others. We also have to present it in such a way that those who are not experts can understand. By having students teach the class, they are going to have to become experts. Not only that, gifted students have a vast array of knowledge and skills that their age-mates may not possess. Giving them a venue to share this will improve not only their retention of that information, but also their public speaking as well as organizational skills.

This might look like an inquiry project. You start with a key topic: for example, space. From that, students generate a list of keywords concerning the topic, such as *universes, planets, comets, moons, NASA, solar system, sun, exoplanets, stars,* etc. Based on their interests, students are flexibly grouped. There might be some groups with five people; there might be a single person interested in a topic. The point is that they get a choice in what they are going to be teaching.

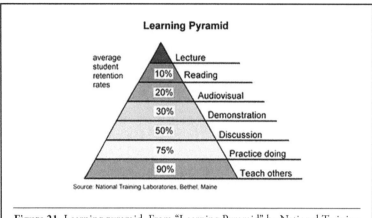

Figure 21. Learning pyramid. From "Learning Pyramid" by National Training Laboratories, n.d., retrieved from http://www.ntl.org. Copyright by National Training Laboratories. Reprinted with permission.

Students then become experts on the topic, building on knowledge they already possess. They can research, interview experts, read books, and watch videos, to learn the material well enough in order to teach it. Throughout this process, they will write learning objectives that they plan on teaching others. Students should have three to five learning objectives. They might look like this for black holes:

1. What causes black holes to form?
2. What do black holes do?
3. What are some black holes that have been discovered?

Then, you push students to create a learning objective with no clear answer—one where they will have to take what they learned and hypothesize, such as: What would happen if a black hole formed in our solar system?

Students then set out to find a way to teach these learning objectives in whatever creative way they can come up with. They could create learning centers, give a presentation, or facilitate a hands-on learning activity. Students would then have performance days to teach their lessons. It is best to provide an estimation of the time allotted for each presentation, so that students know to include enough material to teach the concepts but don't include so much detail that they take too long.

These do not need to be inquiry projects. You could take a few chapters from the textbook and divide students into groups, each one covering a chapter and teaching it to the rest of the class. By having them teach the class, you are helping students learn the content at a deeper level and develop an enduring understanding.

Conclusion

Learning centers, blended learning, and students as teachers are all strategies that can be used in the regular classroom to engage gifted students. Because there is choice, students have some say in their schoolwork and can use their gifts in creative ways. These are good alternatives to a lack of programming or trained teachers but are by no means a replacement. This is no substitute for proper gifted programming and highly trained gifted intervention specialists in challenging and engaging gifted students.

If you would like to read more in-depth about one of these strategies, a good resource is *Differentiating Instruction With Centers in the Gifted Classroom* by Julia L. Roberts and Julia Roberts Boggess.

Cause 9

NOT BEING CHALLENGED

Nothing causes underachievement faster than not being challenged. If a student feels like the work is too easy or that it does not engage him, he is just going to shut down. If a student runs into enough classes where he is not being challenged, underachievement begins to settle in.

You can challenge students in numerous ways. One way is with content. We often do this with mathematics classes, moving students through a progression of new math concepts each year. Because students usually are not exposed to higher level math in their real lives, it is new and fresh to them, which makes it a challenge. If a student is not feeling challenged, we can accelerate him into a math where he will be. Another way to challenge students is through the depth in which the lesson is taught. If you are covering a broad topic such as fractions, how deep can you go into that? How do you get students to think about fractions in different ways and challenge them to use them in various situations? You can challenge students with the method of delivery. Teachers are beholden to teach the standards of a given grade in a given subject area, but they are not told *how* to teach them. Using strategies such as project-based learning, inquiry-based learning, station rotations, blended learning, and others can increase the rigor of the content. You can vary instruction to meet students' needs. You can also challenge students with choice. Allowing students to be part of the decision-making process when it comes to an assignment or assessment creates buy-in. It also can challenge the students because many times the students will create something more difficult than the teacher would have because they are more familiar with their limitations and potential. The topic, form of assessment, delivery method, and others can be choices for the students to make. Creativity can also be used to challenge students. Giving them a lesson where they have to make a creative product allows them to use talents other than just their intelligence. Finding talents that students possess and helping to channel them into their product can produce amazing results.

When the Solution Is Giving Gifted Students More Work

Oftentimes, if a student finishes her work early, the teacher simply gives her more work. This is a problem. No matter how smart she is, no one loves more work. In fact, by virtue of her giftedness, she is smart enough to figure out that if she finishes early, the teacher will give more work, so she begins to slow down and finish with the rest of the class. This is where boredom and lack of challenge begin to rear their ugly heads.

The key is not to assign more work, but to assign *different* work. In fact, the gifted student might end up doing less work than the typical student if you assign the most difficult tasks first:

» When assigning a lesson, discern what material represents the most difficult aspects of what you are asking them to learn.

» Choose five aspects you feel represent mastery of the lesson.

» Students who attempt the most difficult first and answer all parts correctly do not have to complete the rest of the assignment.

» Those who fail to meet the criteria should complete the whole assignment.

Then, what do you do with a student who does finish his work early? You cannot just let him sit there, can you? Numerous strategies have already been shared, such as independent research projects (see p. 110) and passion projects (see p. 116). One of the strategies offered in this chapter is the corners project. This is something that can be used with students who finish work early. Keep in mind this should be a choice. Additional work should be something the student wishes to take on because you have piqued his curiosity and love of learning.

When Higher Level Thinking Is Not Encouraged

Bloom's taxonomy categorizes questions into six different levels of thinking (see Figure 22). Remember, understand, and apply are the lower levels of thinking. They are the basic building blocks of learning and require a lot of rote memorization. If a teacher is to get her gifted students thinking at a higher level, she must use these as a starting point and continue on with the higher level thinking of analyze, evaluate, and create.

How do you push gifted students to this higher level of thinking? By becoming familiar with the verbs of Bloom's taxonomy to the point where you are able to take any question and turn it into a higher level question. By using the verbs in your day-to day activities, you can increase the level of thinking in your classroom. Table 9 shows verbs for each of the levels of Bloom's taxonomy.

You need to be careful. Just using a higher level verb does not elevate a question. For example, if you use the verb *deduce* from the analysis level of Bloom's in a question such as, *Deduce the nouns in the following sentence: The quick fox jumped over the lazy dogs*, you are not asking students to actually analyze. Instead, students are applying their understanding of what a noun is—a person, place, or thing—and identifying those in the sentence. The verb has to match up with the rest of the question to be reaching the higher levels of Bloom's.

A better question would be: *Deduce whether the sentence still makes sense if you switch the nouns in the following sentence: The quick fox jumped over the lazy dogs.* Here, gifted students have to do all of the things they did before. They must understand what a noun is and then identify which words fall into that category. But there is an additional step. Students must analyze their new sentence: *The quick dogs jumped over*

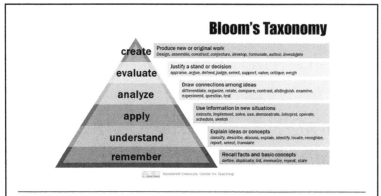

Figure 22. Bloom's Taxonomy. From "Bloom's Taxonomy" by Vanderbilt Center for Teaching, 2016, retrieved from https://cft.vanderbilt.edu/guides-sub-pages/blooms-taxonomy. Used under Creative Commons Attribution 2.0 Generic.

TABLE 9
Bloom's Verbs

Remember	choose, define, find, how, identify, label, list, locate, name, omit, recall, recognize, select, show, spell, tell, what, when, where, which, who, why
Understand	add, compare, describe, distinguish, explain, express, extend, illustrate, outline, paraphrase, relate, rephrase, summarize, translate, understand
Apply	answer, apply, build, choose, conduct, construct, demonstrate, design, develop, experiment with, illustrate, interpret, interview, make use of, model, organize, plan, present, produce, respond, solve
Analyze	analyze, assumption, categorize, classify, compare and contrast, conclusion, deduce, discover, dissect, distinguish, edit, examine, explain, function, infer, inspect, motive, reason, test for, validate
Evaluate	appraise, assess, award, conclude, criticize, debate, defend, determine, disprove, evaluate, give opinion, interpret, justify, judge, influence, prioritize, prove, recommend, support, verify
Create	build, change, combine, compile, compose, construct, create, design, develop, discuss, estimate, formulate, hypothesize, imagine, integrate, invent, make up, modify, originate, organize, plan, predict, propose, rearrange, revise, suppose, theorize

the lazy fox. Then, they have to determine whether it still makes sense. An argument could be made for both:

>> *For*: Yes, the sentence still makes sense because dogs have the ability to jump and foxes can certainly be lazy. My dog, Beckham, is always jumping over the fence in our yard, so I have seen this firsthand.

>> *Against*: No, the sentence doesn't make sense anymore because foxes do not chase after dogs—it is the other way around. Plus, multiple dogs would have to be able to jump over this single fox. He would probably figure out what was going on after a couple had jumped over him.

Notice the pattern of multiple possibilities for answers. That is the difference between lower and higher level thinking questions; lower level questions usually have a single answer, and everyone has to give that same answer in order to be correct. Higher level questions have multiple acceptable answers. This is where the thinking takes place. Gifted students are allowed to think outside of the box.

When Differentiation Is Lacking

Differentiation is like a teacher spinning plates. She gets all of the plates going and then one begins to wobble. She turns her attention to it, helps it get going again, only to find another plate is wobbling. She rushes to that one, gets it the help it needs, only to find another one waning. This is what she does the entire day, preventing plates from falling off their poles and crashing to the ground. She is attending to any plate that wobbles, seeking to get it back on track. The problem is those plates that continuously spin—without ever starting to wobble—never get any attention. Sure, they slow down, but because she never sees them struggle, the teacher does not feel the need to give them her attention. They just spin, never going as fast as they can, but managing to get by.

Oftentimes, with a classroom full of varying abilities, the teacher only has so much attention to give. Students who are struggling are the ones who get the most of her attention, but the gifted students who understand the lesson at a basic level are fine using their intelligence to get by. But gifted students have needs just like the other students—they just might not be as obvious. The help they need looks very different than the help the teacher is giving to struggling students.

Differentiation is a lot of work. In many cases, the teacher aims her attention at the middle, helping to get those struggling to that point, and if other students are already there, not pushing them far beyond. The really skilled teacher is able to work with these wide ranges, helping those students who are struggling, and pushing the gifted students to a higher level, but it is a very delicate balancing act.

Practical Solutions

Strategy 1: Gifted Seminars

There is not a lot of gifted programming at the high school level. This happens for a few reasons. Because students have a choice of classes in high school, if a student feels ready to take an advanced science class or precalculus, she can sign up and take classes that are challenging to her. On the flip side, students can choose not to challenge themselves and simply take the bare minimum courses in order to receive credit. A second reason is there are already advanced and rigorous courses offered through national programs, such as Advanced Placement (AP) and College Credit Plus (CCP). Because these courses are designed to be at a college level, they are far more challenging than the regular fare. A third reason is not too many high schools put students on teaching teams. It is more like a free-for-all, where students can pick and choose the courses they want to take, and they are placed in these classrooms based on the expertise of the teacher. Because of this, it would be nearly impossible to place students on teams with the same students because everyone's schedule is unique. Thus, it would be difficult to cluster students or to create a magnet team of gifted.

With all of these choices, high school seems like it would be very appealing for a gifted child. The issue is that advanced courses are something an intrinsically motivated child would choose. For the gifted student who does not like to challenge himself, or who is turned off by school, there has to be alternative programming that would entice him into still getting enrichment without having to take an advanced class.

One way to do this is through the use of gifted seminars. Gifted seminars are a lot more fluid than a regular class. They are not beholden to the content standards, so a variety of topics could be addressed. Not only that, seminars can be fluid in length as well. They could be a one-time session, last several weeks, or even be held throughout the school year. The seminars should be something that would attract students who might not like school but who are intellectually curious. The seminars could be once a week or every day for a quarter. They could be held in the morning before school begins, after school, or during a common lunch or enrichment time.

For example, a one-time seminar might bring in guest speakers to offer an expertise or life story of interest to students, such as inviting a representative from Amnesty International to come in and talk about what the organization does. Other examples might include:

>> a foreign-born speaker who shares her perspective on the culture of the United States;
>> two guest speakers who are on opposite sides of a debate, such as someone who is for gun restriction and someone who supports the Second Amendment;
>> a professional who can offer an idea of what the profession holds for students, such as a pharmacist, engineer, or reporter;
>> local citizens who might have something to share, such as folks from the senior center who can relay the history they have experienced, local veterans who can share their experiences in the military, or even politicians who might be able to discuss an issue the city is currently facing;
>> university personnel who can talk to students about financial options for college or majors available; or
>> bankers who can talk about managing money and investing.

The seminars could be ongoing, where a topic is covered over several weeks. Topics could include teaching study skills that will come in handy in college or a 21st-century survival skill, such as public speaking, adaptability, entrepreneurialism, problem solving, or collaboration. Nontraditional topics might also interest students, such as a seminar on the songs of Bob Dylan or how Harry Potter has influenced popular culture.

Here is an example of a film studies seminar that could be offered over the course of a year:

>> *The Gold Rush* (1925), starring and directed by Charlie Chaplin; silent film.

>> *Gone With the Wind* (1939), starring Clark Gable, Vivien Leigh, and Olivia de Havilland, directed by Victor Fleming; epic.

>> *Red River* (1948), starring John Wayne and Montgomery Clift, directed by Howard Hawks; Western.

>> *Rear Window* (1954), starring Jimmy Stewart, Grace Kelly, and Raymond Burr, directed by Alfred Hitchcock; thriller.

>> *West Side Story* (1961), starring Natalie Wood, Rita Moreno, George Chakiris, and Russ Tamblyn, directed by Jerome Robbins and Robert Wise; musical.

>> *Jaws* (1975), starring Richard Dreyfuss and Roy Scheider, directed by Steven Spielberg; thriller.

>> *The Little Mermaid* (1989), directed by Ron Clements and John Musker; animated.

>> *Titanic* (1997), starring Leonardo DiCaprio and Kate Winslet, directed by James Cameron; big budget film.

>> *Iron Man* (2008), starring Robert Downey, Jr., and Jeff Bridges, directed by Jon Favreau; superhero film.

>> *The Visit* (2015), directed by M. Night Shyamalan; horror.

Each movie could be shown over the course of a few weeks along with discussion about the genre it represents and how it influenced film upon its release.

Or you could have a more hands-on seminar that runs a simulation over the course of several weeks, such as a stock market simulation. The first seminar would be an explanation of how the stock market works, presented by a teacher or an expert. Then, students would be put into groups and get to choose a series of stocks. Each subsequent week would be spent looking at how their stocks performed over the course of the week and how much money they lost or made. The simulation would look something like Figure 23.

You can be creative with the way you offer seminars. They can be taught by staff members who have a real passion for the topic, outside instructors who have an expertise, or by gifted students themselves. You could even have students submit seminar ideas with a course outline. If their seminar is picked, the student will be allowed to teach it.

Strategy 2: Teaching Higher Level Questioning Skills

One of the most effective ways to help gifted students reach their potential is by creating a culture where there is higher level thinking going on in all aspects of the classroom. In order to do this and build capacity, you must have a good grasp of what higher level thinking is. A good place to start is by showing what higher level thinking is not. A lot of times teachers think the harder the question, the more it will challenge students to think. This is absolutely not true. Asking students to calculate the sum of 2 + 2 is a simple application-level question. If you ask students to calculate the sum of 959,583,583,950 + 245,959,285,929,582, you have made the question harder, but they are still employing the lower level thinking skill of application. You are not challenging students to think at a higher level.

By slightly changing the question, however, you can tap into a higher level of thinking: *Is there a time when 2 + 2 does not equal 4?* Now you are asking students to analyze and evaluate this situation. Analyzing 2 + 2, students can think of situations where it might not equal 4. Then, they must evaluate their answer and convince others. Students might reach the conclusion that 2 + 2 does always equal 4, but must justify this with examples:

>> A student who knows a little bit of advanced math might make the argument that using a Modulo 3 system (which works like a watch) of (0, 1, 2), 2 + 2 actually equals 1 because 2 is the highest possibility, and we are adding the next two numbers, which are 0 and then 1.

Stock Market Simulation Game

- Each group is going to be investing in the stock market.
- Will create a portfolio of five stocks.
- How much stocks lose or gain determines which is the most successful investment group.
- Will run the simulation for 9 weeks.

Rules of Stock Simulation Game

- Every group begins with $10,000.
- Have to select 5 stocks the group is going to invest in.
- Can buy as many shares of the stock as you choose, as long as the total does not reach more than $10,000 and you have at least one share per stock.
  - Want to come as close to $10,000 as possible.
  - What you do not spend the first week is gone.

- Can dump at least three of your stocks and pick up others in the course of the week.
  - 5% fee for every stock dropped and bought.
  - Not every share.

- Report results of the week, which will be recorded on the portfolio sheet with share values, profits, and losses.
  - Must keep your own portfolio. Keep track of your stock value from week to week and whether it has lost or gained.

- Will keep track of all the weeks. Whoever has the best portfolio at the end of the 9 weeks wins.
- Using resources such as *The Wall Street Journal* online, have students choose their first five stocks and figure out their portfolio.
  - Will record these on their stock portfolio sheet.
  - Will not fill out the ending value yet. Just the beginning value.
  - Come as close to $10,000 as possible.
  - Write down next to the name of the stock its abbreviation because some papers do not write out the entire name.
  - Also write down where you got it from:
    - American Stock Exchange
    - Nasdaq
    - New York Stock Exchange

Figure 23. Sample stock market simulation.

Stock Portfolio

Name of Investment Group _____

Week of Portfolio _____

Name of Stock/Company _____ # of Shares _____

Beginning Value	Ending Value	Gain/Loss
$	$	$
$	$	$
$	$	$
$	$	$
$	$	$
	Total Profit/Loss	$
	Past Weeks Totals	$
	Portfolio Total	$

Figure 23. *Continued.*

» Or a student could make the argument that 2 + 2 is using the nominal measurement scale. The nominal scale simply names or classifies. Each number, rather than representing a number, represents a category or individual, such as numbers on football uniforms. Having the number 2 on your uniform does not necessarily mean you are the No. 2 athlete on your team. There is no numerical value to that assignment. Instead, it is merely an identifier. Locker numbers are also nominal. Each number is a unique qualifier that distinguishes one locker from another.

» A student could even make an argument that 2 + 2 does not equal 4 but instead equals ballet (because you wear a tutu while dancing).

There is not just one answer. There are countless possibilities for gifted students to think about. But, whatever decision a student makes, he must justify his answer. This causes him to tap into a higher level of thinking and will stretch and grow his brain, improving his ability to think critically.

To help get you started on asking higher level questions, you can use what are called openers:

Analyze:
- » What conclusions can you draw about . . . ?
- » What is the relationship between . . . ?
- » How is _____ related to . . . ?
- » What inferences can you make about . . . ?
- » What assumptions do you make about . . . ?

Evaluate:
- » Compare two characters in the selection. Which was a better person. Why?
- » Which character would you most like to spend the day with?
- » How could you determine . . . ?
- » Why was it better that . . . ?
- » Would it be better if . . . ?

Create:
- » What would happen if . . . ?
- » What changes would you make to . . . ?
- » Suppose you could _____. What would you do?
- » How would you rewrite the section from _____'s point of view?
- » How would you rewrite the ending of the story?

Getting better at asking these sorts of questions will take practice. The important thing is you keep trying. A good indicator you are not asking higher level questions is the student can answer is in a single sentence or by writing just a few words. If you are asking these questions correctly, it should lead to a rich discussion or a detailed response.

You will want this higher level thinking to become the culture in your classroom. Part of that involves revisiting your assessments. Look them over, and ask yourself, are half of these questions higher level . . .

even a quarter . . . any? If they are not a good mix of lower and higher level questions, then you will want to consider revising your assessments. Are there lower level questions that can be turned to higher level with just a few changes and a different verb? For example, here is a lower level question found in many ELA classes: *How does the setting influence the story?* This question checks a student's ability to recognize through comprehension where the book is set. There is definitely a right and a wrong answer, but if you want a gifted student to think critically about the setting, you would be better served asking: *If the setting were different, would this change the effectiveness of the story in any way?* This question allows the gifted student to recognize and identify the setting but also to create a setting of his own.

Here is a social studies question: *What are three factors that allowed the colonists to win the American Revolution?* This question checks a student's ability to recall facts. These facts may be very complex and involved, but they are still something she was told or read, and she is repeating them back. To get her to think critically, you might ask: *How might the United States be different if the British had won the American Revolution?* This question requires her to take knowledge and understanding she has accumulated and make a likely prediction based on these (e.g., British people drink a lot of tea, but colonists stopped drinking tea to protest the taxes and started the Boston Tea Party. Thus, Americans might not drink as much coffee and would drink more tea.).

In addition to asking and writing questions that are higher level, daily student assignments can also use the various level of Bloom's taxonomy. An example of this would be a lesson using the story of Goldilocks and the Three Bears:

> » *Remember*: List the items used by Goldilocks while she was in the Bears' house.
> » *Understand*: Explain why Goldilocks liked Baby Bear's chair the best.
> » *Apply*: Demonstrate what Goldilocks would use if she came to your house.
> » *Analyze*: Compare this story to reality. What events could not really happen?

> » *Evaluate*: Judge whether Goldilocks's actions were good or bad. Defend your opinion.
> » *Create*: Propose how the story would be different if it were Goldilocks and the Three Fish.

There are six activities for students to do, each at a different level of Bloom's. You could do this in various ways. You could have all students do all six activities, choose three activities, or rotate through stations involving each of the activities. You could assign groups depending on ability, clustering your gifted students together, having the higher groups do the higher levels of Bloom's with others doing the lower levels.

Strategy 3: Corners Projects

The corners projects are the perfect answer to: *What do I do with students when they finish early?* A project, along with its requirements, resources, and any other materials that might be needed, is placed in each corner of the room that is designated as a workspace. The corners projects are not necessarily tied to the curriculum, but are designed to enrich students by being engaging lessons. The projects should be intriguing enough to students that their curiosity and love of learning will entice them want to work on them if they get done early. The projects should be designed so that a student could work for 15 minutes on it and then put it away, only to pick it up another time she finishes her work early. The projects should all have creative products that the student can produce to show mastery. New projects can be rotated in every grading period or, if popular, used throughout the year. Because there are various ways the students could approach the projects, they could work on the same project twice and produce very different results.

An example of corners projects in an elementary or middle school English language arts classroom is shown in Figure 24.

Corner #1: Seuss on the Loose

Brief Description

You will read a collection of Dr. Seuss books and determine the theme of the stories. Even though Seuss is using wild characters and creatures, what point is the author trying to get at? You will also be looking at Seuss's use of rhyme to tell a story.

Product

After finding the theme of several books, you will apply it to a situation in your own life and similar situations you might face. You will eventually write your own Dr. Seuss-like book that shows this theme.

Skill

Determine the theme and whether it is implied or stated directly.

Starting Point

The Sneetches and Other Stories by Dr. Seuss

Suggested Materials

Various Dr. Seuss books, such as:
- *The Butter Battle Book*
- *Thidwick: The Big-Hearted Moose*
- *Horton Hears a Who*
- *The Lorax*
- *Did I Ever Tell You How Lucky You Are?*
- *Oh, the Places You'll Go!*

Corner #2: Autobiography

Brief Description

They say everyone has a story to tell, and you will tell the one about your life. This will include your family history, a timeline of important events in your

---

Figure 24. Sample corners projects for an elementary or middle school English language arts class.

own personal history, how your family came to be in Ohio, and events that have shaped who you are.

Product

You will write an autobiography that chronicles your life. You may want to include a timeline that shows the history of your family and/or a family tree that indicates the family lineage.

Skill

Create paragraphs with topic sentences and supporting sentences (that are marked by indentation and are linked by transitional words and phrases).

Construct timelines with evenly spaced intervals for years, decades, and centuries to show the order of significant events.

Starting Point

Talk with your parents about your family tree and create one using an online family tree creator such as Family Echo.

Suggested Materials

Supplies to make a 3-D family tree and timeline

Corner #3: And They Lived Happily Ever After . . . Or Did They?

Brief Description

Have you ever wondered what happened to characters after a book ends? Does their story continue even if a sequel does not come out? Here you will take a book or character and continue the story, predicting what might happen in the future.

Product

You will write a short story that continues the original story, showing what might happen to the characters after the book ends.

Figure 24. *Continued.*

Skill

Write narratives that sequence events, including descriptive details and vivid language to develop plot, characters, and setting and to establish a point of view.

Starting Point

Read *Goldilocks Returns* by Lisa Campbell Ernst.

Suggested Materials

- Paper
- Original story
- Imagination

Corner #4: Magnetic Poetry

Brief Description

Magnetic poetry is taking words that are printed on magnets and arranging them into a poem. A prefix is an affix attached before a base word or root, as *re-* in *reprint,* while a suffix is an affix attached to the end of a base, root, or stem that changes the meaning or grammatical function of a word, as *-en* added to form *oxen.*

Product

Here you will make your own poem using at least 10 prefixes and 10 suffixes, identifying the prefixes and suffixes used.

Skill

Identify the meanings of prefixes, suffixes, and roots and their various forms to determine the meanings of words.

Starting Point

Read some examples of poetry provided.

Suggested Materials

- Small pieces of paper
- Directions for how to use

Figure 24. *Continued.*

Conclusion

The best way to challenge a student is by offering choice. An underachieving gifted student is much more apt to learn something if he is choosing to do so than if it is being assigned. One might argue that school is not about having choice; school is about what you are supposed to learn. But, if we want to create lifelong learners, we need to instill in them this desire to learn. The best way to accomplish this is to make them care about what they are learning through choice.

If you would like to read more in-depth about one of these strategies, a good resource is *Questioning Strategies for Teaching the Gifted* (The Practical Strategies Series in Gifted Education) by Elizabeth Shaunessy-Dedrick.

Cause 10

BEING TOO SMART FOR THEIR OWN GOOD

Is there such a thing as being *too gifted*? When one looks at a highly gifted individual like Bobby Fischer, it causes one to wonder. Bobby Fischer was a chess prodigy, who, at 14, became the U.S. Chess Champion and then the only American World Chess Champion at age 29. Some of the quirks that made him unique, however, also caused him to ostracize himself from the game. He refused to defend his World Championship when the governing body would not relent to his sometimes ridiculous requests. He eventually became a recluse, living in Iceland, spiraling further and further into erratic behavior.

As a child, Ted Kaczynski had an IQ of 167 and was accepted to Harvard at the age of 16. He got his doctorate in mathematics but, at age 29, moved to a remote cabin in Montana without running water or electricity. He then spent the next 18 years mailing homemade bombs to individuals under the guise of the Unabomber.

Clearly, these are two extreme examples of highly gifted individuals gone wrong. Not every super genius is going to end up descending into madness, but there are certainly challenges to being much smarter than the general population (Lebowitz, 2016):

> » You often think instead of feel.
> » People frequently expect you to be a top performer.
> » You might not learn the value of hard work.

» People might get annoyed that you keep correcting them in casual conversation.
» You understand how much you don't know.
» You tend to overthink things.

Many of these have been discussed previously, but the one that trips up many gifted students is overthinking. Their brains run at such a rapid pace they do not see Occam's razor, a problem-solving strategy that suggests the simplest solution is oftentimes the best. On a multiple-choice test, a student with advanced thought processes might attempt to rationalize how any of the choices could be correct. Or a highly gifted child working in a group of students might want to discuss and debate the merits of the group's choices while everyone else thinks they have a solution and want to move on. Sometimes a gifted student can be his own worst enemy.

When Perfectionism Strikes

Perfectionism is more common in gifted students than in typical students. This is not necessarily a bad thing. Having high expectations and wanting what you are working on to be your best work can lead to some positive results (NAGC, n.d.a):
» doing the best you can with the time and tools you have,
» setting high personal standards with a gentle acceptance of self, and
» not allowing behaviors to interfere with daily life (Sec. 1).

The issue is not that the child wants to be perfect. Issues arise when she allows the perfectionism to cause her to freeze her ability to do anything until she believes it to be perfect. Examples of unhealthy perfectionism are (NAGC, n.d.a):
» emphasizing and/or rewarding performance over other aspects of life;
» perceiving that one's work is never good enough;
» feeling continually dissatisfied about one's work;

>> feeling guilty if not engaged in meaningful work at all times; and

>> having a compulsive drive to achieve, where personal value is based on what is produced or accomplished (Sec. 2).

When perfectionism gets in the way of productive achievement and generally being happy, it becomes a social-emotional issue that can affect academics. A student might stare at a test, terrified to put anything down for fear of making a mistake. As a result, she does not finish the test. Or, a student gets feedback from the teacher, but he cannot take the criticism and use it constructively. Instead, he sees it as a condemnation of his work and himself.

Sometimes perfectionism can be a combination of a student wanting to be perfect and the high expectations of parents. If a parent accepts nothing lower than an A, there is not much room for error, so the student thinks he needs to be perfect. There are things the teacher and parents can do to help students cope with perfectionism (NAGC, n.d.a):

>> model a healthy approach and be aware of the student's predispositions toward compulsive excellence;

>> refrain from setting high, non-negotiable standards;

>> emphasize effort and process, not results;

>> do not withhold support or encouragement if goals are not met; and

>> focus on positive self-talk (Sec. 3).

Recognizing a student has the tendency to be a perfectionist is half the battle because then you can offer the help and support the student needs when you see the symptoms arise.

When Other Issues With Too-Smart Children Arise

People will often joke that they suffer from obsessive-compulsive disorder (OCD) because of a little quirk they have, such as wanting to be sure their hands are constantly clean or feeling compelled to take that one pencil that is pointing downward and turning it so it matches the others. OCD, however, is a very serious condition that can cause one to become impaired or distressed. It is not as simple as a quirk. It is a repetitive behavior that the person feels compelled to do. Sometimes it can be seen by others, such as flipping a light switch up and down 37 times each time you leave a room, but other OCD can be internal, such as repeating a phrase over and over again in your mind. Here are some characteristics and examples of behavior of students who are gifted and have OCD (Caccamise, 2013):

>> *Fear of contamination*: The student is always cleaning up and/ or washing and rewashing her hands; she might have dry, chapped, cracked, or bleeding hands that may resemble eczema.

>> *Fear of harm, illness, or death, or pathological doubting*: The student is always checking things; he has a compelling urge to return home to check on something or is constantly checking his locker and/or backpack.

>> *Symmetry*: The student is often arranging; she might tie her shoelaces until both look identical, duplicate steps from one place to another, and/or arrange books on a shelf until they appear symmetrical.

>> *Number*: The student counts, repeatedly counting up to a particular "magic" number.

>> *Scrupulosity (fear of doing or having done something evil)*: The student seeks penance, repetitively saying mental prayers or mantras (p. 2).

OCD can interfere with a student's ability to perform where he is capable. There are strategies a teacher can take to help students cope with OCD (Caccamise, 2013):

>> Teach students about learning strategies (i.e., breaking work up into chunks, using a laptop for writing).

>> Help students identify strategies that work for them (i.e., seating arrangements, allowing them a permanent bathroom pass).

>> Help students set short-term goals.

>> Set small steps to accomplish a task (i.e., taking a test, writing a story, completing math assignments).

>> Emphasize students' strengths and help them work on their weaknesses.
>> Look for triggers.
>> Develop cues with students that will help them refocus (you might even have a safe place for them to go).
>> Be flexible with deadlines (p. 2).

Again, it takes the eye of a knowledgeable teacher to recognize when a student might be struggling with their impulses and defusing the situation. The teacher should not be disciplining the student for having these behaviors; rather he should be figuring out a way to work with her so that she can use her gifts.

When Abstract Thinkers Cannot Develop Concrete Answers

The gifted mind can be very adept at thinking in an abstract manner, which means gifted students are often able to reflect on ideas. You might hear them say, "I wonder . . . " or, "What if this happened . . . ?" They are able to think about situations that are not present, but other students may only be able to think about what is right in front of them. Abstract thinkers:

>> are able to use metaphors and analogies with ease;
>> can understand the relationship between both verbal and nonverbal ideas;
>> possess complex reasoning skills, such as critical thinking and problem solving;
>> can mentally maneuver objects without having to physically do it, known as spatial reasoning;
>> are adept at imagining situations that have happened or are not actually happening; and
>> appreciate sarcasm.

Abstract thinking is great when you are having discussions, working on design challenges, or sharing new ideas, but it does not always translate well to traditional assessment. Many assessments require concrete thinking, and these types of students can sometimes find it difficult to make the translation from abstract to concrete. As a result, they struggle in a traditional classroom with its emphasis on the concrete. There are other classroom environments that are much more nurturing, where there are open-ended questions, encouragement of creative solutions, and instances where students can give their opinion rather than just an answer. If abstract thinkers are not blessed with a classroom such as this, school can be a struggle and underachievement begins to settle in.

When Students Only Know How to Play the Game of School

As discussed, some gifted underachieving students are not willing to play the game of school (see p. 108). On the other hand are students who know how to play the game of school so well that they get out of ways to challenge themselves. These are students who know exactly what they have to do in order to get a good grade in a class but are not willing to go above and beyond that. This student will do her homework, turn in assignments, and, for all those observing, seem compliant. This student, however, is not giving it her all. She is an efficiency expert, doing the bare minimum in order to succeed. She is not willing to challenge herself, and, if the teacher runs a classroom where there is no challenge, this student is perfectly fine with this.

For these types of students, it is hard to argue with their logic. Why work hard and take chances when you could be getting the same grade, or even a better one, by doing exactly what is asked of you and playing it safe? These students are smart enough to do what is necessary to get a good grade, but they lack accuracy in their work. Accuracy involves:

» craftsmanship of work, or quality;
» communicating the answer clearly;
» learning for learning's sake, not just getting it done;

» persistence for fidelity;
» taking pride in your work; and
» setting high standards.

Ideally, you want all students to strive for accuracy, but especially gifted students, because otherwise they are not going to grow as learners. If they set the minimum standard or concern themselves with just completing a task, they are not going to be tapping into their potential. In order to grow as learners, students have to do more than just allow the teacher to challenge them; they must figure out ways to challenge themselves.

Practical Solutions

Strategy 1: Activities That Translate Abstract to Concrete

Translating the abstract to the concrete can be difficult for some gifted students. Consider the saying, "See the forest for the trees." If someone can see the forest for the trees, he can see the big picture. This same person, however, might not be able to describe a single tree in detail. Abstract thinking is about the big picture, but concrete is much more specific. Take, for example, love, an abstract concept. It means very different things to very different people. And one's definition of love evolves over time. When you are a child, you love your parents and your toys. When you get older, you love your spouse or your children. There are, however, very concrete examples of love:

» an elderly couple celebrating their 50th anniversary,
» a baby snuggling with her stuffed teddy bear,
» a couple exchanging their wedding vows,
» a man in his 40s waxing and caring for his sports car, or
» a woman finding the perfect pair of shoes for a reasonable price.

In order to get students to go from the grandiose ideas that are swirling about in their heads to something they can put on a page, you have to engage them in lessons that allow them to access abstract thinking. One way to take thinking from abstract to concrete is to interpret paintings. Take, for example, Vincent van Gogh's *Starry Night*. Have students create a story based on the painting. Some students might choose to focus on the little town off in the distance, some might make the mountain in the foreground the setting, or those science fiction fantasy fans might have the story taking place within the night sky. Regardless of where they set the story, students must visualize something specific, starting to think in a concrete manner.

The same can be done interpreting poetry, which is usually very abstract. Have the students find the concrete. Consider "This Is Just to Say" by William Carlos Williams. Although the imagery is very concrete, there is some abstractness. Who is the poem for? The title suggests that the author is telling it to someone. Who is the author talking to? What is his relationship with the person he addresses in the poem?

You can also take the abstract to the concrete in math. Math has a lot of abstract concepts. Just the act of learning to count has many abstract qualities to it. Students must take these abstract mathematical concepts and create concrete answers. One way to do this is through the use of manipulatives, items you can touch and move around that allow a student to count, figure out fractions, discern patterns, and complete other math tasks. These include blocks, shapes, base 10 blocks, Unifix cubes, fraction bars, and plastic counting cubes. They can also be everyday objects used to aid in the learning of math. Using manipulatives in the math classroom with underachieving gifted students can help them bridge the gap from abstract to concrete thinking.

Strategy 2: Goal Setting

Setting goals allows students to see the finish line not as some far-off aspiration that seems too difficult to accomplish, but rather as short tasks. If you were told you had to run a marathon, that would seem like a daunting task, but if it was broken up into 26 one-mile increments, it seems more achievable.

It can be as simple as breaking a long book into sections to read:

The Grapes of Wrath—Due date March 13
Week 1: Read pages 1–115.
Week 2: Read pages 115–230.
Week 3: Read pages 231–345.
Week 4: Read pages 346–464.

The goal is to have read a certain amount of pages so the student does not have to read the entire book in a few days because she procrastinated. The goal can be more complex and involve breaking a long-term project into shorter goals:

History Research Paper—Due September 24
Week 1: Conduct research on the railroad.
Week 2: Write rough draft of paper.
Week 3: Continue writing the rough draft.
Week 4: Type the final draft.

In both of these cases, the goal is completion. You can also have students set quality goals. It is not as simple as, "Get an A on a test." There needs to be an action plan as to how that is going to happen. You have to set incremental goals called benchmarks:

Day 1: Review notes with a highlighter.
Day 2: Rewrite important concepts from notes.
Day 3: Create index cards with important terms.
Day 4: Have Mom quiz me over index cards.

Each goal builds on the one before and involves a specific action that leads to the final goal. It is a blueprint for how to achieve the goal that if a student followed, she would be most likely be successful.

Depending on how much guidance a student needs, you can use a daily goal sheet to ensure that the student is on track. A weekly goal sheet might look like Figure 25.

Week 1

Day 1

Goal by the end of the day: _____

How I plan to achieve this goal: _____
_____
_____

Verification that I achieved this goal (teacher/parent/peer signature):

_____

Day 2

Goal by the end of the day: _____

How I plan to achieve this goal: _____
_____
_____

Verification that I achieved this goal (teacher/parent/peer signature):

_____

Day 3

Goal by the end of the day: _____

How I plan to achieve this goal: _____
_____
_____

Verification that I achieved this goal (teacher/parent/peer signature):

_____

Figure 25. Sample weekly goal sheet.

Day 4

Goal by the end of the day: _____

How I plan to achieve this goal: _____

_____

_____

Verification that I achieved this goal (teacher/parent/peer signature):

_____

Day 5

Goal by the end of the day: _____

How I plan to achieve this goal: _____

_____

_____

Verification that I achieved this goal (teacher/parent/peer signature):

_____

_____

Figure 25. *Continued.*

Strategy 3: Time Management Skills

Time management is a 21st-century survival skill every student could benefit from. It is especially effective with gifted students who are underachieving due to overthinking. Some students either wait until the last minute to complete a project, because in the past they were able to get away with it, or they think they have little to no chance to pull it off in the time allotted. Being able to manage time allows students to take very big ideas and chunk them into smaller parts, making them more manageable.

One strategy is backward building. A student starts the project by envisioning what the ideal final product will look like. Backward building uses a model established by Wiggins and McTighe (2005): First, students identify what will be accomplished, then they determine what product will best show what they have learned, and finally they plan how they will develop and execute the product.

For example, a student has been assigned a project where she has to prepare an experiment for the science fair. She has been given 4 weeks to accomplish the task, and the end product is a trifold display that she presents. Looking at the big picture, this may seem like a daunting task, but by backward building and breaking it into smaller chunks, it becomes very manageable. The student envisions what the project will look like at the end: *Present project to visitors at the Science Fair.* Working backward, the student determines what she must complete in the step before the last. She will probably want to practice her presentation so it sounds rehearsed and professional: *Practice Science Fair presentation.* Before she can practice, however, she will need to have created her display that describes her work: *Create trifold display with steps and results of the experiment.* The student continues until she has created a series of steps that will lead her to the final product:

>> Present project to visitors at the Science Fair.
>> Practice Science Fair presentation.
>> Create trifold with steps and results of the experiment.
>> Draw a conclusion about your experiment (Did it meet the hypothesis?).
>> Conduct experiment.
>> Gather supplies for the experiment.
>> Create a hypothesis of what the outcome will be.
>> Research the experiment to understand the science behind it.
>> Decide on what the experiment is about.
>> Brainstorm possible ideas for the science experiment.
>> Understand what the scientific method is and how to use it.

Now that this student has broken this large project into smaller tasks, the next step is estimating how long each of these steps will take. For example, conducting the experiment may take 10 days, while creating the trifold might only take 3, whereas gathering supplies might only take 2 days. Remind your student this is only an estimate. She might only take 2 days to research the science behind the experiment but may find she needs more time to get her trifold ready. The schedule is not written in stone, but it does provide checkpoints for the student to notice if she is behind schedule. If she finds herself an entire week behind, she is not managing her time well, and she will need to adjust accordingly in order to catch up.

To aid with time management, a calendar might be a good resource (see Table 10). Without these periodic deadlines, students may wait until the last moment to try to do everything. Whenever the teacher sits down to conference with a student, it is helpful to look at the calendar to chart the progress. A calendar allows students to break the project into parts, making it more doable, and helps them to see the steps necessary to complete the project.

Conclusion

Because a very intelligent child's brain is running a mile a minute, it is important to develop strategies that focuses it and slows it down. This can aid a child who suffers from OCD, perfectionism, or has difficulty translating the abstract into the concrete, and who might otherwise descend into underachievement.

TABLE 10

Sample Calendar

1 Understand the basic steps of the scientific method.	**2** Understand how to use these steps.	**3** Figure out how I am going to use these steps in my own experiment.	**4** Brainstorm ideas of what I'd like to do an experiment on.	**5** Narrow down my brainstorming to just a few choices for my science experiment.
6 Choose what I want my experiment to be about	**7** Begin to research the topic of my experiment.	**8** Continue to research the topic of my experiment.	**9** Research to understand how I am going to apply my topic to the scientific method.	**10** Create a hypothesis for my science topic.
11 Gather my supplies for the experiment (ask Mom if you need to buy any).	**12** Day 1 of my experiment (record findings in journal).	**13** Day 2 of my experiment (record findings in journal).	**14** Day 3 of my experiment (record findings in journal).	**15** Day 4 of my experiment (record findings in journal).
16 Day 5 of my experiment (check hypothesis to see if it is holding up).	**17** Day 6 of my experiment (record findings in journal).	**18** Day 7 of my experiment (record findings in journal.)	**19** Day 8 of my experiment (record findings in journal).	**19** Day 9 of my experiment (record findings in journal).
20 Day 10 of my experiment (record findings in journal).	**22** Draw conclusion about the experiment (did hypothesis hold up?).	**23** Plan for trifold and how I want it to look (get a trifold as well).	**24** Create trifold that shows the steps of the scientific method I used.	**25** Continue working on trifold that shows the steps of the scientific method I used.
26 Continue working on trifold that shows the steps of the scientific method I used.	**27** Finish up trifold that shows the steps of the scientific method I used.	**28** Write the presentation for my science fair experiment.	**29** Practice the presentation for my science fair experiment.	**30** Science fair event.

Part III

CONCLUSION

When Gifted Students Reach Their Potential

When you profile an underachieving gifted student, you should be looking at his needs. It should not be about which issues are holding him back, but instead the needs you can meet in order for him to succeed.

Let us take a look at the five examples we discussed before:

» Albert Einstein, who suffered from boredom;
» Eminem, who had a poor home life;
» Dylan Klebold, who faced problems with his peers;
» Winston Churchill, who had a lack of trained teachers; and
» Agatha Christie, who was twice-exceptional.

Imagine if Einstein had had a teacher who allowed him to work on independent research projects, would he have cracked that time travel theory of his? Or, if Eminem had had a poetry slam club to go to after school, would he have developed into a rapper at a much faster pace? If Dylan Klebold had been put into a magnet program, would he have found peers that were more like-minded and not have been influenced by Eric Harris?

Gifted underachievers have similar profiles: They are not using their gifts to the best of their ability. Unique to them, however, is the strategy (or strategies) to correct their underachievement. That might mean trying more than one and finding the right fit for the right child. Remember that one size does not fit all, and it is not the student who must conform to the teacher but the other way around.

The strategies that were shared in this book are not limited to the cause of underachievement they were associated with. Magnet programs can do wonders for the social-emotional needs of students. Passion projects can be used with bored students as well as those lacking intrinsic motivation. Higher level questioning skills can help any gifted child access his or her critical thinking ability. And time management would benefit twice-exceptional students, as well as those with a poor home life. The important thing is to have a variety of tools in your toolbox, so when you come across an underachieving gifted student in your classroom, you can fix the problem with the proper tool.

The Power of Caring

The strategies are designed to help a gifted child use his gifts and, as a result, reach his potential. In addition to implementing strategies to combat underachievement, remember the importance of the student feeling as though someone cares about him. Obviously you care enough about your students to have picked up this book and read this far.

I know the importance of this caring, not just because of my 20 years working with gifted students. I know this importance because I was that underachieving student in high school. All through elementary and middle school, I was an exemplary student, wanting to please the teacher and score high marks. I got pulled out for a special science class for advanced students in elementary school and had a math teacher in sixth grade who let me work at my own pace, allowing me to get through the entire textbook in the first quarter. Then, for some reason in junior high, I stopped caring about my grades. Instead, I became an efficiency expert. I learned that if I did not do my homework and did well enough on the test, which I would not study for, I could end up with a C in the class. This was still passing. There were some classes such as English and social studies where I was more motivated by the subject matter, so I tended to get B's, but my math and science classes were a disaster. I was either reading a Stephen King book while the rest of the class took notes, or I just slept in class. Why did I sleep in class? My teachers let me. No one said a word to me concerning it. Because no one seemed to care, I did not care, and thus I would get more sleep in school than I would during the night. I was always compliant, however. If my teacher asked me to do something, I would do it. The problem was my teachers were not asking much of me, so that is what I gave them.

Then, during my senior year I had a teacher who suddenly cared if I slept in her class. The second I put my head down the first time, she asked if I was feeling all right and if I needed to go to the nurse's office. Her words seemed to show she cared, but her tone showed she was not going to tolerate someone sleeping in her class. Because of this, I never attempted again to sleep in her class. Besides, I could get caught up on my snoozing in my government and zoology classes. This caused me to pay attention more, which resulted in better grades. Imagine that. I also had a math teacher who motivated me to do something I had never done in my high school math career—get an A. This teacher cared so much about math that it was infectious, rubbing off on the students and making them care about it. I had gotten D's in algebra II my junior year, and here I was in trigonometry getting A's. This was not because his class was easier. On the contrary, it was much more challenging than any other math class I had taken, but the math teacher I had the year before never seemed enthusiastic about the math. She never seemed to care, so I did not care about it either. My senior year, I got the best grades I ever received in my junior high and high school career. Better late than never, I guess.

I often reflect back on that time and wonder, what if I had not had those two teachers who cared my senior year? What if, like many of the other teachers I had, she did not mind if I slept in class or he did not seem to care about his subject matter? Would I have gone to college riding this wave of confidence and have been as successful as I was? Would I have gotten into college at all?

Because of this, I have always had a special place in my heart for students like Mike, whose story I shared at the beginning of the book. I recognized there was something more there because I had been like him when I was in junior high. It just took the right teacher to see me not as a student who was challenging, but as someone who needed to be challenged. Regardless of how Mike's vocational life played out, I am very proud of him. I still have a book of poetry he created with a fellow classmate when he was in high school and a CD of his band's lone, self-produced album. My primary goal as an educator is to help the likes of Mike, the likes of me, and any student who has the gifts to reach that potential. No saying is truer to me than the one that claims a mind is a terrible thing to waste.

In addition to this book, I have created a picture book, *The Unopened Gift*, available at https://myedexpert.com/vendor/twosox21. It is an allegory of the gifts that so many students possess but are unwilling to open. Use it to spark conversations with students no matter their age. Use it with parent groups to jumpstart a conversation about the underachievement they may see in their own child. Use it with fellow educators to try to recognize underachievement amongst their students and what might be the causes for this. Use it to start a conversation about the importance of opening one's gifts and using them.

References

Amato, P. R. (2005). The impact of family formation change on the cognitive, social, and emotional well-being of the next generation. *The Future of Children, 15*(2), 75–96.

American Psychiatric Association. (2013). *Diagnostic and statistical manual of mental disorders* (5th ed.). Washington, DC: Author.

American Sociological Association. (2011). Bullying victims often suffer academically, particularly high-achieving blacks and Latinos. *ScienceDaily.* Retrieved from https://www.sciencedaily.com/releases/2011/08/110823104844.htm

Baum, S. M., Schader, R. M., & Owen, S. V. (2017). *To be gifted and learning disabled: Strength-based strategies for helping twice-exceptional students with LD, ADHD, ASD, and more* (3rd ed.). Waco, TX: Prufrock Press.

Besnoy, K. D. (2006). Successful strategies for twice-exceptional students. In F. A. Karnes & K. R. Stephens, *The practical strategies series in gifted education.* Waco, TX: Prufrock Press.

Betts, G., & Neihart, M. (1988). Profiles of the gifted and talented. *Gifted Child Quarterly, 32,* 248–253.

Bryner, J. (2007). Most students bored in school. *Live Science.* Retrieved from https://www.livescience.com/1308-students-bored-school.html

Bumpass, L. L., & Sweet, J. A. (1989). Children's experience in single-parent families: Implications of cohabitation and marital transition. *Family Planning Perspectives, 21,* 256–260.

Caccamise, R. C. (2013). *Teaching students who are gifted and OCD?* Retrieved from http://lcps.k12.nm.us/wp-content/uploads/2013/02/Teaching-Students-who-are-Gifted-and-Obsessive-Compulsive-Disorder.pdf

Callahan, C. M., Moon, T. R., & Oh, S. (2014). *National surveys of gifted programs: Executive summary.* Charlottesville, VA: National Research Center on the Gifted and Talented, University of Virginia.

Center for Comprehensive School Reform and Improvement. (2008). *Issue brief: Gifted and talented students at risk for underachievement.* Washington, DC: Learning Point Associates.

Cohn, A., & Canter, A. (2003). *Bullying: Facts for schools and parents.* Retrieved from http://www.naspcenter.org/factsheets/bullying_fs.html

Covey, S. (2014). *The 7 habits of highly effective teens.* New York, NY: Touchstone.

Davidson Institute for Talent Development. (2009). *What's new in gifted education.* Retrieved from http://news.ditd.org/June_09/eNews_June_09_web.htm

Delisle, J. (2006). *Parenting gifted kids: Tips for raising happy and successful children.* Waco, TX: Prufrock Press.

DeNeen, J. (2013). 10 reasons why educators should encourage independent learning. *informED.* Retrieved from http://www.open colleges.edu.au/informed/news/teachers-or-facilitators-10-reasons-why-educators-should-step-out-of-the-way-and-encourage-independent-learning

DoSomething.org. (n.d.). *11 facts about bullying.* Retrieved from https://www.dosomething.org/facts/11-facts-about-bullying

Dowdall, C. B., & Colangelo, N. (1982). Underachieving gifted students: Review and implications. *Gifted Child Quarterly, 26,* 179–184.

Duckworth, A. (2016). *Grit: The power of passion and perseverance.* New York, NY: Scribner.

Fletcher, A. C., Steinberg, L., & Sellers, E. B. (1999). Adolescents' well-being as a function of perceived interparental consistency. *Journal of Marriage and the Family, 61,* 599–610.

Fonseca, C. (2016). *Emotional intensity in gifted students: Helping kids cope with explosive feelings* (2nd ed.). Waco, TX: Prufrock Press.

Genius Hour. (2017). *What is genius hour?* Retrieved from http://www.geniushour.com/what-is-genius-hour

Gladwell, M. (2008). *Outliers: The story of success.* New York, NY: Little, Brown.

Gordon, S. (2016). 8 ways bullying affects gifted students: Why gifted students are targeted. *Verywell*. Retrieved from https://www.verywell.com/how-bullying-impacts-the-gifted-student-460594

Grotzer, T. (n.d.). *The keys to inquiry*. Retrieved from https://web.archive.org/web/20160611231625/http://hea-www.cfa.harvard.edu:80/ECT/Inquiry/inquiryintro.html

Hanushek, E. A. (1997). Assessing the effects of school resources on student performance: An update. *Education Evaluation and Policy Analysis, 19,* 141–164.

Hébert, T. P. (2011). *Understanding the social and emotional lives of gifted students*. Waco, TX: Prufrock Press.

Hidden Angel Foundation. (n.d.) *Multi sensory environments: The benefits*. Retrieved from http://www.cdhaf.org/multi-sensory-environments-the-benefits

Hoffman, J. L., Wasson, F. R., & Christianson, B. P. (1985). Personal development for the gifted underachiever. *Gifted Child Today, 8*(3), 12–14.

Huffington Post. (2011). *Bullying victims see lower GPAs, particularly high achieving blacks and Latinos, study shows*. Retrieved from http://www.huffingtonpost.com/2011/08/23/bullying-victims-see-lowe_n_933988.html

Individuals with Disabilities Education Act, 20 U.S.C. §1401 et seq. (1990).

Kell, H. J., Lubinski, D., & Benbow, C. P. (2013). Who rises to the top? Early indicators. *Psychological Science, 24,* 648–659.

Kim, C. (2008). Academic success begins at home: How children can succeed in school. *The Heritage Foundation*. Retrieved from http://www.heritage.org/education/report/academic-success-begins-home-how-children-can-succeed-school

Lebowitz, S. (2016). 6 surprising downsides of being extremely intelligent. *Business Insider*. Retrieved from http://www.businessinsider.com/downsides-of-being-smart-2016-7

Lee, S. Y., Olszewski-Kubilius, P., & Thomson, D. T. (2012). Academically gifted students perceived interpersonal competence and peer relationships. *Gifted Child Quarterly, 56,* 90–104.

Levy, S. (2011). *In the plex: How Google thinks, works, and shapes our lives*. New York, NY: Simon & Schuster.

Linsin, M. (2012). 8 things teachers do to cause boredom. *Smart Classroom Management*. Retrieved from http://www.smart classroommanagement.com/2012/01/28/8-things-teachers-do-to-cause-boredom

Lips, D. (2008). *A nation still at risk: The case for federalism and school choice*. Retrieved from http://www.heritage.org/education/report/nation-still-risk-the-case-federalism-and-school-choice

Lubinski, D., Webb, R. M., Morelock, M. J., & Benbow, C. P. (2001). Top 1 in 10,000: A 10-year follow-up of the profoundly gifted. *Journal of Applied Psychology, 4,* 718–729.

Manzone, J. (2014). Learning centers: A strategy to differentiate instruction for the 21st century class. *Gifted Education Communicator*. Retrieved from http://giftededucationcommunicator.com/gec-fall-2014/learning-centers

McCall, R.B., Evahn, C., & Kratzer, L. (1992). *High school underachievers: What do they achieve as adults?* Newbury Park, CA: SAGE.

Meyers, S. A. (2009). Do your students care whether you care about them? *College Teaching, 57,* 205–210.

National Association for Gifted Children. (n.d.a) *Perfectionism*. Retrieved from https://www.nagc.org/resources-publications/resources-parents/social-emotional-issues/perfectionism

National Association for Gifted Children. (n.d.b) *Social & emotional issues*. Retrieved from https://www.nagc.org/resources-publications/resources-parents/social-emotional-issues

Neihart, M. (2000). Gifted children with Asperger's syndrome. *Gifted Child Quarterly, 44,* 222–230.

Peterson, J. S. (2000). A follow-up study of one group of achievers and underachievers four years after high school graduation. *Roeper Review, 22,* 217–224.

Peterson, J. S., & Ray, K. (2006). Bullying and the gifted. *Gifted Child Quarterly, 50,* 148–168.

Post, G. (2015). *Underachievers under-the-radar: How seemingly successful gifted students fall short of their potential* [Web log post].

Retrieved from http://giftedchallenges.blogspot.com/2015/11/underachievers-under-radar-how.html

Reis, S. M., Neu, T. W., & McGuire J. M. (1995). *Talents in two places: Case studies of high ability students with learning disabilities who have achieved.* Storrs, CT: University of Connecticut, The National Research Center on the Gifted and Talented.

Renzulli, J. S., Reid, B. D., & Gubbins, E. J. (1992). *Setting an agenda: Research priorities for the gifted and talented through the year 2000.* Storrs: University of Connecticut, The National Research Center on the Gifted and Talented.

Richert, E. S. (1991). Patterns of underachievement among gifted students. In J. H. Borland (Series Ed.), M. Bireley, & J. Genshaft (Vol. Eds.), *Understanding the gifted adolescent* (pp. 139–162). New York, NY: Teachers College Press.

Rimm, S. B. (1986). *Underachievement syndrome: Causes and cures.* Watertown, WI: Apple.

Rimm, S. (2008). *Why bright kids get poor grades and what you can do about it: A six-step program for parents and teachers* (3rd ed.). Tucson, AZ: Great Potential Press.

Robbins, A. (2006). *The overachievers: The secret lives of driven kids.* New York, NY: Hyperion.

Robinson, F. P. (1970) *Effective study.* New York, NY: Harper & Row.

Rogers, K. B. (1991). *The relationship of grouping practices to the education of the gifted and talented learner* (RBDM9102). Storrs, CT: University of Connecticut, The National Research Center on the Gifted and Talented.

Siegle, D. (2006). The emotional edge: Parenting strategies to motivate underachieving gifted students. *Duke Gifted Letter, 4.*

Siegle, D., & McCoach, D. B. (2001). Promoting a positive achievement attitude with gifted and talented students. In M. Neihart, S. M. Reis, N. M. Robinson, & S. M. Moon (Eds.), *The social and emotional development of gifted children: What do we know?* (pp. 237–250). Waco, TX: Prufrock Press.

Silverman, L. K. (2007). Perfectionism: The crucible of giftedness. *Gifted Education International, 23,* 233–245. doi:10.1177/026142940702300304

Silverman, L. K. (2011). *The moral sensitivity of gifted children and the evolution of society. Supporting Emotional Needs of the Gifted.* Retrieved from http://sengifted.org/the-moral-sensitivity-of-gifted-children-and-the-evolution-of-society

Stanley, T. (2012). *Project-based learning for gifted students: A handbook for the 21st-century classroom.* Waco, TX: Prufrock Press.

Stanley, T. (2014). *Performance-based assessment for 21st-century skills.* Waco, TX: Prufrock Press.

Stanley, T. (2017). *10 performance-based projects for the language arts classroom: Grades 3–5.* Waco, TX: Prufrock Press.

Steenbergen-Hu, S., Makel, M. C., & Olszewski-Kubilius, P. (2016). *What one hundred years of research says about the effects of ability grouping and acceleration on K–12 students' academic achievement: Findings of two second-order meta-analyses.* Retrieved from https://www.ctd.northwestern.edu/blog/what-one-hundred-years-research-says-about-ability-grouping-and-acceleration-students-k-12

StudentMentor.org. (2017). *Benefits of mentorship.* Retrieved from http://www.studentmentor.org/how-it-works/mentee-and-mentor-benefits

Szabos, J. (1989). Bright child, gifted learner. *Challenge, 34.*

Thompson, J. (2016). *6 blended learning models: When blended learning is what's up for successful students.* Retrieved from https://elearningindustry.com/6-blended-learning-models-blended-learning-successful-students

Trilling, B., & Fadel, C. (2009). *21st-century skills: Learning for life in our times.* Hoboken, NJ: Jossey-Bass.

Tsatsoulis, P. (2002–2017). *The effects of pushing academics too hard. Brainy-Child.* Retrieved from http://www.brainy-child.com/article/pushing-academic.shtml

Vanderbilt Center for Teaching. (2016). *Bloom's taxonomy.* Retrieved from https://cft.vanderbilt.edu/guides-sub-pages/blooms-taxonomy

VanTassel-Baska, J. (1992). *Planning effective curriculum for gifted learners.* Denver, CO: Love.

Weiss, L. (1972). Underachievement—empirical studies. *Journal of Adolescence, 3,* 143–151.

Whitmore, J. F. (1980). *Giftedness, conflict, and underachievement.* Boston, MA: Allyn and Bacon.

Whitmore, J. R. (1986). Preventing severe underachievement and developing achievement motivation. In J. R. Whitmore (Ed.), *Intellectual giftedness in young children: Recognition and development.* New York, NY: Haworth Press.

Whitmore, J. R. (1989). Re-examining the concept of underachievement. *Understanding Our Gifted, 2*(1), 10–12.

Wiggins, G., & McTighe, J. (2005). *Understanding by design* (2nd ed.). Alexandria, VA: Association for Supervision and Curriculum Development.

Winebrenner, S., & Brulles, D. (2008). *The cluster grouping handbook: How to challenge gifted students and improve achievement for all.* Minneapolis, MN: Free Spirit.

About the Author

Todd Stanley is the author of 10 teacher education books, including *Project-Based Learning for Gifted Students: A Handbook for the 21st-Century Classroom* and *Performance-Based Assessment for 21st-Century Skills*, as well as the 10 Performance-Based Projects series. He was a classroom teacher for 18 years, working with students as young as second graders and as old as high school seniors, and was a National Board Certified teacher. He helped create a gifted academy for grades 5–8, which employed inquiry-based learning, project-based learning, and performance-based assessment. He is currently the gifted services coordinator for Pickerington Local School District, OH, where he lives with his wife, Nicki, and two daughters, Anna and Abby.